SACRED
PLACES

FOR SPIRITUAL ADVENTURERS
EVERYWHERE

SACRED PLACES

WHERE TO FIND WONDER IN THE WORLD

aster

CLARE GOGERTY

CONTENTS

Page 2: Castlerigg stone circle, Cumbria, England.
Opposite above: Holy and venerated: Varanasi, India.
Opposite middle: Mysterious and unknown: Es Vedrà, Ibiza.
Opposite below: Sacred and potent: Uluru, Australia.
Overleaf: The Sacred Valley, Peru, where Incan Emperors ruled.

WHAT MAKES A PLACE SACRED?

There are certain places in the world that hold an inexplicable magic. Either stumbled upon or actively sought, they have the power to stir something within us; something profound and memorable that is beyond the everyday. This feeling can be hard to describe, but it is instantly recognizable, immediately familiar. Ancient and eternal, it is the same emotion that moved our distant ancestors and prompted them to build stone circles, construct temples and carve monumental statues. The Ancient Greeks understood about the power of place – they had two words for space: *topos* described its physical characteristics, *chora* its mysterious or poetic qualities. Sacred places have an abundance of *chora*.

A remote temple, Phu, Nepal.

Defining sacred places is an elusive business. A sense of wonder can arise in many different locations, from visiting a Mayan pyramid, entering a Buddhist shrine, walking through a forest, ascending a mountain, or dipping your fingertips into a holy spring. One way to identify a place as sacred is simply by the emotional response stirred within you by its distinctive atmosphere.

Reasons for visiting sacred places are as diverse as the sites themselves. We might be driven there by the need to escape the humdrum of our daily lives and to seek adventure, or be pulled there by history, myth and legend. Our own beliefs and faith may propel us to visit somewhere of meaning to us. We may seek a powerful, peaceful place in which to meditate and discover more about ourselves. Or we could simply be curious to see what a place looks like and to experience it emotionally and spiritually.

The growth in "meaningful" travel has seen more of us looking for a spiritual depth to our wanderings. Increasing numbers of us are seeking a holiday that delivers on another level. A journey to a place of meaning provides a destination and a purpose. It also reveals much about the history, myths and culture of the country. As Paul Devereux writes in *The Sacred Place*: "These places offer a respite from the secular world. Sometimes we need holidays for our souls, not just for our bodies and mind."

Whether it's an ancient tree in a local park or a magnificent temple in Bali, visiting a sacred place is an opportunity to take time out and walk away from our hurried lives with their insistent demands. It gives us the space to connect with something beyond our own self, and in turn to reconnect with ourselves.

Opposite: St Nectan's Kieve waterfall, Cornwall, UK.

A GUIDE TO TRANSFORMATIONAL TRAVEL

There are moments in our daily lives that give us an inkling of how we can change. A yoga class can awaken a sense of mindful movement and a desire to learn more. A walk in a forest can trigger a realization of the power of nature and the need to spend time outdoors. A meditation app might prompt us to investigate a spiritual path. Watching a super moon rise above the rooftops can instigate a yearning to connect more deeply with the natural world.

With the realization that change is possible comes the call to action. Listen to that call and the journey begins. Travel has always been said to broaden the mind, but just relocating yourself from one place to another and taking a few snaps won't change you. A newer way of travel – transformational travel – goes deeper. It's about reflection and self-development, a greater communion with nature, culture and spirituality. It's an inner journey as well as an outer one, and it's an ongoing process: the journey continues when you get home.

Transformational travel is often prompted by a significant, life-changing moment – the end of a relationship, perhaps, or leaving a place of work. It's at times of personal crisis that we look around us to find

ways to change. Leaving the comfortable, known world and setting off on a purposeful adventure is one way to do it. That may mean choosing to spend a week on a yoga retreat, or following an ancient pilgrimage route, or deciding to learn more about Buddhism by spending time at a monastery. It is a different way to engage with the world and the people in it. It gives travel more meaning.

The effectiveness of the transformational journey is proved when we get home. Some kind of internal shift, personal growth or deepening of self-awareness has taken place. We behave differently and make alterations to our lives. These can be small adjustments or significant changes – a move to another country, say, or the adoption of a new religion.

An inner change has occurred that will last long after the physical journey has ended.

Above: The sacred city of Jerusalem. Opposite: Pine Tree Island, Japan.

STEPS ON YOUR TRANSFORMATIONAL JOURNEY

1 LISTEN TO THE CALL:
Is there a place that beckons you? Or are you on a spiritual quest, a search for meaning? Be aware of places and ideas that resonate with you. Follow their call, who knows where they may take you?

2 PREPARE FOR THE JOURNEY:
Research the places that you intend to visit – use this book as your starting point! Draw up a loose itinerary, but leave plenty of space for spontaneity.

3 STEP OVER THE THRESHOLD:
The planning is over, the journey begins.

4 TRAVEL WITH INTENTION & MINDFULNESS:
Leave with the intention to learn wisdom from cultures that are not your own. Engage your mind, senses and emotions as you wander. Really see what's in front of you. Stop often to reflect on what you have seen. Greet people with openness. Step lightly and leave little impact. Be a participant, not a spectator. Pay attention. Record your experiences in a journal.

5 RETURN HOME & REFLECT:
Consider what your journey has meant and how it has changed you. Honour your courage for being so adventurous and be grateful for the opportunities it has provided.

6 CONTINUE TO CHANGE:
Take action and apply what you have learned to your daily life. Keep evolving. The outer journey may have ended but the inner journey is just beginning.

WAYS TO PROMPT TRANSFORMATION

- Stay in an ashram and practise yoga.
- Walk around a mountain, not up it.
- Learn to chant with Buddhist monks.
- Practise meditation on a holy mountain.
- Learn tai chi in a monastery.
- Attend a religious festival and participate in it.
- Learn about different faiths in their country of origin.
- Walk a pilgrimage route.
- Consider going on an ayahuasca retreat (see Central & South America, page 190).
- Travel alone.
- Walk more and do so mindfully.
- Listen to the land.
- Attend a gong bath at a spiritual retreat.
- Forest bathe.
- Celebrate the solstice at a stone circle.
- Swim in a sacred river.
- Be cleansed in a hot spring.
- Make an offering at a temple.
- Wash your face in a holy spring.

Opposite: Two Tibetan Buddhist nuns in Kathmandu, Nepal.

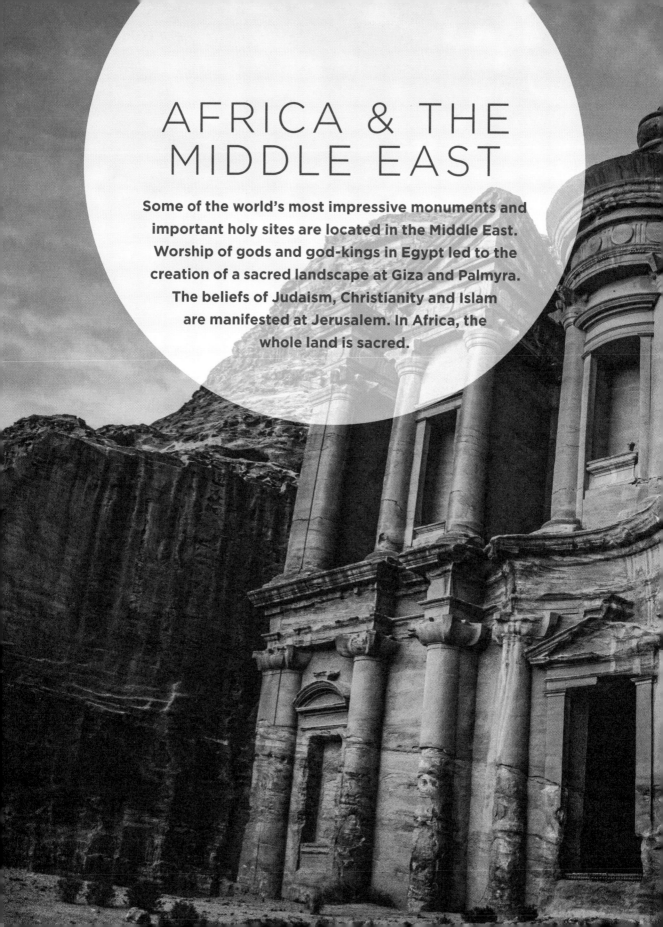

AFRICA & THE MIDDLE EAST

Some of the world's most impressive monuments and important holy sites are located in the Middle East. Worship of gods and god-kings in Egypt led to the creation of a sacred landscape at Giza and Palmyra. The beliefs of Judaism, Christianity and Islam are manifested at Jerusalem. In Africa, the whole land is sacred.

THE TEMPLE OF HATHOR

DENDERA TEMPLE COMPLEX, QENA, EGYPT

THE WONDER OF IT

On the west bank of the Nile between Luxor and Abydos, Dendera, a magnificent, sacred complex, stands alone in the desert. At its heart is a temple dedicated to Hathor, one of Ancient Egypt's most revered goddesses. Intricately decorated with hieroglyphs, colourful carvings and reliefs, it is suitably impressive for a goddess held in such high esteem.

A MULTI-PURPOSE SACRED SPACE

The joy of exploring Dendera is largely because it is so well preserved. Walk through the Temple of Hathor's grand entrance and among the 24 monumental carved columns of its Great Vestibule, and you get a sense of what it must have been like for Hathor's devotees arriving to honour their favourite deity. You can almost feel the press of worshippers and their gasps of wonder as they came to her statue in the temple's sanctuary, to be healed in the sacred pool, to pay their respects at ancestors' tombs, or to give birth in the *mammisi* (birthing temple).

Built between 54 and 20 BCE by Ptolemy XII and Cleopatra VII, the Temple of Hathor comprises a series of rooms, each intricately adorned with figures of emperors, pharaohs and deities, plus screeds of hieroglyphs. There are chambers, crypts, shrines to various gods, and the sanctuary to marvel at. The wealth of intricate decoration on the walls and ceilings continues from room to room.

A climb up a spiral corridor leads to the top of the temple where, in a small temple, rituals were held to greet the rising sun. Another chapel dedicated to Osiris has a relief of a circular zodiac on its ceiling, thought to be the only representation of the Ancient Egyptian sky during the age of Pisces over 2,000 years ago. (It is a copy of the original, which is in the Louvre in Paris, France.)

The passage to the underground crypt requires a certain amount of stooping, but it is worth it to see the "Dendera Lightbulb". The similarity of this carved relief to a modern bulb led some to conclude that Ancient Egyptians had knowledge of electrical technology. It's more likely however that it represents a *djed* pillar (a common Egyptian symbol representing stability), a lotus flower and a snake (symbolizing fertility). Alongside it is a portrait of sky god Horus, who was the son and consort of Hathor. The birthing temple at the front of the complex is also rich with decoration, mostly depicting the births of gods and pharaohs, and the small chapel behind the Temple of Hathor has a damaged relief of Isis giving birth.

There were more festivals in Ancient Egypt devoted to Hathor than any other god, and she was worshipped in temples throughout the country. Her temple at Dendera, however, is the most splendid.

Opposite above: A sandstone capital of the Goddess Hathor.
Opposite below: Carved stone wall panels in the Dendera Temple.

HATHOR GODDESS GUIDE

Hathor was the Egyptian sky goddess of fertility, love, music and dancing. She was commonly called "the golden one", and texts found at her temple at Dendera say that "her rays illuminate the whole earth". Hathor was one of the most popular goddesses in Ancient Egypt: a cult grew around her and more temples were devoted to her than to any other goddess. Unusually, male and female priests both operated in her temples and there were also musicians, midwives and dream interpreters.

GIZA PLATEAU

CAIRO, EGYPT

THE WONDER OF IT

On the outskirts of Cairo lies the world's most acclaimed and mysterious graveyard. Dominating the plateau, an extension of the necropolis at Memphis, is the Great Pyramid, the tomb of the pharaoh Khufu. Beside it are two smaller pyramids (one where Khufu's son Khafre is entombed; the other the tomb of Khafre's son Menkaure). Keeping guard over all of them is the Sphinx, an incredible monument carved from a single piece of rock.

TO INFINITY & BEYOND

The Giza Plateau is more than a memorial to the dead. The site was designed as a departure point to propel the spirits of kings into the afterlife. To get them there involved orientating the pyramids to align with the stars: a complex and mathematical process requiring sophisticated surveying skills.

THE GREAT PYRAMID: GATEWAY TO THE GODS

The scale of the Great Pyramid – its base covers 5 hectares (13 acres); it comprises 2,000,000 limestone blocks and is 147m (482ft) high – makes it impressive enough today. But when it was built more than 4,000 years ago, its dazzling coat of limestone would have made it overwhelmingly magnificent. This massive tomb for the pharaoh Khufu was not merely a place to bury and glorify him: it was built to propel him into the afterworld. The King's Chamber (where his body lay entombed) has four vents in the north and south faces. Belgian engineer Robert Bauval calculated that in 2500 BCE, the southern air vent of the King's Chamber would have pointed directly at Orion. He also found that the southern shaft of the Queen's Chamber beneath it would have pointed at the star Sirius (the star sacred to Osiris' consort, Isis). These astronomical alignments could have been intended as a channel to direct Khufu to Orion, where he would become a god. A ritual was held to coincide with the moment of greatest alignment, so that Khufu could be shot into orbit like a cannonball.

Giza is about a 30-minute drive from Cairo and can be easily accessed by car or as part of a group tour.

A MAP OF THE HEAVENS

The Ancient Egyptians were exacting astronomers, taking measurements to align their pyramids with north, south, east and west. Using a *merkhet* (an instrument that tracks stars), they also took sightings of constellations, particularly the Great Bear and Orion. They believed that their gods lived in an afterworld called the Duat, where their pharaohs would join them after death. The Duat was the kingdom of Osiris, the god of rebirth and afterlife, and was located in the region of the sky where Orion and Sirius rise ahead of the sun at dawn on the summer solstice.

A compelling, but disputed, theory suggests that the Giza Plateau is a mirror of the Duat: its three pyramids correlate to the position of the three stars on the Belt of Orion; the Sphinx corresponds to the constellation of Leo; and the Nile is a terrestrial representation of the Milky Way. This could be a

Opposite: The Great Pyramid, behind the Sphinx, was the tomb of pharaoh Khufu.

way of creating a sacred landscape that reflected the divine night sky, bringing its energy down to earth.

THE ENIGMATIC SPHINX

This colossal statue with its face of a man and body of a recumbent lion is familiar to most of us today, but for centuries it was buried in the sand. Following excavation in 1925–36, its true size and magnificence was revealed. It is carved from one piece of limestone bedrock, making it the largest single stone statue in the world. Its face is likely to be that of the pharaoh Khufu, whose tomb is in the Great Pyramid; the statue would have been carved to commemorate him at the order of his sons. It sits on an alignment running west to east, carefully positioned to coordinate with the other monuments at Giza.

"He is no longer upon Earth, he is in the sky! He rushes at the sky like a heron; he has kissed the sky like a falcon."
Hymn 682, Ancient Egyptian Pyramid Texts

The face of the Sphinx is likely to have been that of pharaoh Khufu.

PYRAMID POWER

The pyramids on the Giza Plateau outside Cairo are the best known in Egypt, but there are many others – there are estimated to be more than 100 in various states of repair – stretching along the west bank of the Nile. Why this structure, with its quadrilateral base rising to a triangular point, was chosen so often is unknown. Although largely associated with Egypt, pyramids also appear in other ancient civilizations as places of ritual, entombment and ancestor worship. Mud-brick structures, known as ziggurats, were built in ancient Mesopotamia, as well as in Mayan cities throughout Central and South America, and in ancient Greece, Rome and China. Surprisingly, there are more pyramids (255) in Sudan than in Egypt: the royal cemetery in Nuri, on the west side of the Nile, alone has more than 20 pyramid tombs for the kings and queens of the Nubian Kingdom of Kush.

Theories abound about the power of pyramids. It has been said that the shape generates energy, preserves food, sharpens razor blades and boosts plant growth, but nothing has, so far, been scientifically proven.

SAINT CATHERINE'S MONASTERY

SINAI PENINSULA, EGYPT

THE WONDER OF IT

Ancient, sacred and solemn, Saint Catherine's Monastery sits silent and solitary at the foot of one of Christianity's holiest mountains. It is believed that this is where God spoke to Moses and where the angels brought the body of Saint Catherine after she was martyred.

A HOLY PLACE OF PILGRIMAGE

The sand-coloured walls of Saint Catherine's Monastery rise from the rocky wilderness, and for centuries pilgrims arrived at the monastery after a punishing and hazardous journey across the desert. Travelling from Jerusalem, Eilat and Cairo, they were drawn here (and still are) by the holiness of the location, the sacred relics of Saint Catherine and the precious manuscripts and icons housed in the library.

The monastery sits on the slopes of Jebel Musa (Arabic for "the mountain of Moses"), where it is said Moses received the Ten Commandments from God, and where God spoke to him as a burning bush. Many see the monastery as the starting point for an onward pilgrimage to the summit of Jebel Musa. The mountain is also identified as Mount Sinai and is a holy location for Christians, Jews and Muslims. There are two ascents to the top. The older one is up 3,750 steps, carved by a monk, and it is known as the "steps of repentance", passing the Spring of Moses and a chapel dedicated to the Virgin Mary. The other is more circuitous and more gradual. At the summit is a chapel to the Holy Trinity with frescoes that portray the story of the life of Moses, and a 12th-century mosque. It is possible to make the climb to the summit in the early morning to see the sun rise in spectacular fashion over the vast, barren desert.

The history of the monastery itself stretches back to the 3rd century when Empress Helena had a small chapel built at the site of the burning bush. Prayer and worship have taken place here ever since. Walls were built around the original chapel in the 6th century, at the order of Emperor Justinian, to protect the basilica, its monks and Christians seeking refuge.

Today the monastery is in the hands of the Church of Sinai, part of the Greek Orthodox church, and its brothers still carry out daily devotions. As well as the relics of Saint Catherine (off-limits to visitors), a bramble (*Rubus sanctus*) believed to be a transplanted descendant from the actual burning bush, grows in a chamber, the Chapel of the Burning Bush, behind the altar.

SAINT CATHERINE OF ALEXANDRIA

Saint Catherine's symbol – the wheel – is familiar to anyone who has enjoyed a firework display. The story behind the spinning, sparkling Catherine wheel firework, however, has faded from memory over the years.

Legend has it that Saint Catherine was born in Alexandria around 287 CE into a wealthy family. When she was 18, she had a vision and converted to Christianity. With new-found zeal, she condemned the Emperor Maxentius for his persecution of Christians. He tried to silence her by confronting her with 50 pagan philosophers, but she countered all their arguments and even converted some of them. The emperor executed the philosophers for their trouble, then tried to persuade Catherine to marry him in another attempt to subdue her. She refused, saying that she was "a bride of Christ". This enraged him further and he imprisoned her. In prison, Catherine converted many of the Imperial Guard as well as Maxentius' wife, all of whom the Emperor executed.

The only course of action for Emperor Maxentius was to execute Catherine. He prepared a spiked breaking wheel, but when she touched it, it shattered. Thwarted, he instructed that she be beheaded. After her execution, a milky substance flowed from her neck, rather than blood. Angels then took her body to Mount Sinai where it lay until 850 CE, when monks found it, still intact, not having decomposed.

Saint Catherine's feast day is 25 November and she is the patron saint of philosophers, preachers, librarians and young girls.

Above: For centuries, pilgrims walked across the desert to St Catherine's Monastery.

THE NILE

A great river is a life-giving force, and nowhere more so than in the desert. It is easy to understand why the Nile was sacred to the Ancient Egyptians, and why it is still venerated today. All around it is barren wilderness, but along its banks there is greenery, life and nourishment. Survival is not possible without it.

The Ancient Egyptian temple complex at Karnak.

The Nile is formed from two separate tributaries – the White Nile, which flows from central Africa, and the Blue Nile, whose source is in the highlands of Ethiopia. Their confluence is at Khartoum in Sudan, from where the river flows northwards until it splits into a wide delta and empties into the Mediterranean Sea.

Sources of rivers are magical places. The water rises from the earth in a trickle, unassuming and modest, with little suggestion of the mighty torrent it will become. The Blue Nile's sacred source is the three springs in Gish Abay in the foothills of Mount Gish, Ethiopia. Pilgrims travel here to be blessed, to give thanks for the holy water and to seek good fortune or healing. The vast, beautiful water of the inland sea, Lake Tana, has also been nominated as the river's source.

The source of the White Nile is, according to a trio of explorers in 2006, a muddy pool in the Nyungwe Forest in Rwanda.

ANCIENT EGYPTIANS & THE NILE

The Nile was a central part of Ancient Egyptian beliefs. Regarded as the source of life, it was interwoven with the myths and world of the gods. Most of the temples honouring the gods were built along its banks. All tombs were built on its west bank, as it was believed this was the side that symbolized death.

These sacred, cosmological and ancient sites have become a chain of stop-off points on many Nile cruises, and with good reason. Starting from Cairo, you pass the pyramids of Giza (see page 18), then onwards to Karnak on the east bank, the biggest temple complex in the world, grand in scale, with ram-headed sphinxes and a sacred lake, and its neighbouring temple complex at Luxor.

On the other side (the west bank) of the river is the necropolis, with its tombs and monuments including the Valley of the Kings and Valley of the Queens, where pharaohs and their wives were interred. The beautiful temple at Esna, further along, was one of the last built in Egypt and was dedicated to the god Khnum, the god of the source of the Nile (he later became god of rebirth and creation). Downriver, the temple at Edfu, dedicated to Horus, is one of the best-preserved shrines in Egypt and houses the colossal black statue of Horus as a falcon. Kom Ombo is a double temple dedicated to the crocodile god Sobek and the falcon god Haroeris. Finally, the small temple at Philae, dedicated to Isis and other deities, formed the centre of the Ancient Egyptian cults, and was the last pagan temple in use in Egypt.

Opposite: The story of the Nile is interwoven with myths and tales of the gods.

THE OUZOUD FALLS

MOROCCO

CRASHING FALLS

From an amphitheatre of red rocks – the edge of the Atlas Mountains – the Ouzoud Falls power into a pool from a height of 100m (330ft). The narrow muddy track to the waterfalls passes along the El Abid gorge under a canopy of olive trees. Barbary macaques swing by. The falls, of which there are several, crash to the ground, causing rainbows to shimmer into view, and powering flour mills in caves below (*ouzoud* means "grinding grain" in the Berber language).

SACRED WATERFALLS

Shamans and seers from many different cultures regard waterfalls as powerful places to connect with the spirit world as they are gathering points for ancestral souls. Sleeping beside one with the roar of the water pounding in your ears is said to induce prophetic dreams and visions.

The Jivaroan people of Ecuador involve waterfalls in their initiation rituals. The vision seeker walks naked behind the waterfall, chanting. At night they drink potent tobacco water and wait for a vision. If none comes, the process is repeated until one does.

FIVE OTHER WATERFALLS TO FALL FOR AROUND THE WORLD

1 **MOROCCO: CASCADES D'AKCHOUR, CHEFCHAOUEN:** The two waterfalls at Akchour in the Rif Mountains are reached by walking from Chefchaouen for around two hours through a forested gorge. Less visited than the Ouzoud Falls, they are a peaceful place to spend an hour or so.

2 **THE PHILIPPINES: TINAGO FALLS, ILIGAN CITY:** Five cascades framing an emerald-coloured pool, these create a watery and misty veil over fern- and moss-covered cliffs. In a deep ravine reached by a steep staircase, they take a bit of finding, which makes them all the more rewarding.

3 **UNITED STATES: HAVASU FALLS, ARIZONA:** On the reservation of the Havasupai people, in a side canyon of the Grand Canyon, an aqua-blue waterfall spills over orange travertine cliffs. Book a visit in advance and walk the 8-km (5-mile) trail to reach it.

4 **SCOTLAND: FAIRY POOLS, GLENBRITTLE, ISLE OF SKYE:** Blue, crystal-clear pools are fed by waterfalls from the Cullin Mountains. This is a good wild-swimming spot, only accessible via a 2.4-km (1½-mile) walk through the forest from the car park.

5 **LAOS: KUANG SI FALLS, LUANG PRABANG:** A series of cascading tiers flows through prettily shaped limestone pools (some big enough to swim in; some sacred to the local people and off limits) before joining the river.

On returning home, they will dream of the ancestral soul who appeared in the vision, causing the power of that spirit to enter their bodies.

MYTHS & MAGIC: THE LEGEND OF TINAGO FALLS

During her mother's pregnancy, an unborn baby was cursed by an enchantress disguised as a beggar. The baby was born ugly, and her parents – the king and queen – were ashamed of her and hid her in a cave. They called her Tin-ag, which means "hidden face". They continued to care for her, but she never left the cave. As she grew older, she realized how beautiful the world was outside. The enchantress took pity on her and offered her the chance to become something "of great beauty and splendour". The princess agreed and the enchantress turned her into a beautiful waterfall.

Above: The cascading Ouzoud Falls.

OSUN-OSOGBO SACRED GROVE

OSOGBO, OSUN STATE, NIGERIA

THE WONDER OF IT

This dense primary high forest in southern Nigeria is the home of the Yoruba fertility goddess Osun. Shrines, sculptures and art placed to honour her are threaded along the Osun River like sacred beads.

THE HOME OF THE RIVER GODDESS

This sacred grove, located along the banks of the Osun River, was created around 400 years ago to honour Osun, goddess of the Yoruba people of southwestern Nigeria. Among the ancient trees are 40 shrines, two palaces, five sacred places and nine worship points. All have designated priests and priestesses. It is also a natural pharmacy: more than 400 species of plants grow in the forest, many of which are known for their medicinal value.

Sacred groves were once common outside Yoruba towns, but most have vanished or diminished in size.

This one, however, has survived, is the largest of them all and is an active religious site. The annual Osun-Osogbo festival in August attracts thousands of worshippers who come to celebrate the goddess Osun with drumming, dancing and musical performances. The festival begins with a ritual called the Iwopopo, cleansing the town of evil. Three days later, the Ina Olujumerindinlogun, a 600-year-old lamp, is ceremonially lit.

The continued use of the grove for religious worship is due to the unstinting dedication of Austrian artist Susanne Wenger (Yoruba name: Adunni Olorisha). Adopting Osogbo as her home in 1958, she halted the desecration of its shrines, which had led to its priests leaving in the 1950s. By establishing a local artistic community, known as the New Sacred Art movement, she restored the grove and reintroduced sculpture and carvings. Many of these, including her own work, are of various *orishas* (deities or spirits). Others are of natural forms such as flowers and trees. She also rebuilt the shrines, especially those dedicated to Osun. It is a tribute to

her work and talent that the Sacred Grove is now a UNESCO World Heritage Site. Following healing by a Yoruba herbalist, Susanne herself became a Yoruban priestess and was the grove's guardian until she died there, aged 93, in 2009.

To visit, head to the city of Osogbo (a four-hour drive from Lagos); there are few road signs, but everyone in Osogbo will be able to point you in the right direction. Once there an entrance fee is payable (plus an additional fee for taking a camera). You will be accompanied by a guide who can take you into the heart of the forest.

Opposite: Sculptures in the sacred forest at Osun-Osogbo honour the Yoruba goddess Osun.

JERUSALEM

THE SACRED SITES

THE CHURCH OF THE HOLY SEPULCHRE

Although it has moved several times, the Via Dolorosa (Way of Sorrows), a narrow alleyway sneaking through the Old City of Jerusalem, is considered by Christians to be the route that Jesus walked to Mount Calvary. Along its length are the 14 Stations of the Cross, each one signifying a moment on his path to crucifixion. Christians stop and pray at each one. At the end, they reach the Church of the Holy Sepulchre, within which is the rocky cave where Christ was buried and rose from the dead. The Angel's Chapel under the church's dome contains the stone that the angel is said to have rolled away from the entrance to the tomb. Outside the Old City is the Mount of Olives where Jesus, as described in the Bible, ascended to heaven. The Garden of Gethsemane at its foot is where he prayed before his crucifixion.

TEMPLE MOUNT/HARAM AL SHARIF

This paved area which stretches over 57 hectares (140 acres) is sacred to both Muslims and Jews. It is home to two of Islam's most sacred buildings: the Dome of the Rock and the Al Aqsa Mosque, and is revered by Jews as the location of the First Temple and all that survives of their Second Temple – the Wailing Wall.

THE JEWISH SITE/HAR HABAYIT

According to one Jewish tradition, Temple Mount was where God gathered earth to form Adam, the first man. Another says it is where Abraham was asked to sacrifice his son, Isaac. It is certainly an important sacred site.

King David captured Jerusalem in about 1000 BCE, thereby uniting the northern tribes of Israel and the southern tribes of Judea and making the city the capital of the 12 tribes of Israel. Solomon, the son of King David, is said to have erected the First Temple here on the site of his father's altar. He placed the Ark of the Covenant (God's contract with man) inside. After Solomon's death, the tribes of Israel split, and Jerusalem was once more the capital for the tribe of Judea. The temple was destroyed by the Babylonians in 586 BCE.

A Second Temple was built by order of Herod the Great, appointed King of Judea by the Romans in 31 BCE. He built a wall around the Mount and created the plaza. This was in turn destroyed by the Roman emperor Titus in 70 CE. All that survived was the supporting wall of the Temple Mount, which is now Judaism's most sacred shrine: the Western (or Wailing) Wall. For more than 1,000 years, Orthodox Jews have come here to mourn the downfall of the Temples. Sacred scrolls are contained in lockers along the Wall, and pilgrims write personal prayers and slip them into the cracks in the stones.

DOME OF THE ROCK

This, the third holiest place in Islam, after Mecca and Medina, is where, according to Muslim tradition, the Prophet Muhammad started his "night journey" into heaven, from the rock at the centre. As described in the Koran, the Archangel Gabriel appeared to Muhammad one night and presented him with a flying beast, al-Buraq ("lightning"), which carried him from Mecca to Jerusalem. On arrival, he prayed with Abraham, Moses, Jesus and other prophets at the sacred rock, then ascended to heaven on al-Buraq, where Allah instructed him about prayer. He returned to Mecca before morning.

Built in 688–91 CE by the caliph Abd al-Malik, the Mosque was constructed on the site of the Second Temple of the Jews. Although it is one of the oldest examples of Islamic architecture, it has been modified over the centuries. The striking gold dome, which can be seen all over the city, was gold-plated in 1959–60. A shrine inside the Dome of the Rock contains a hair that is alleged to be from the head of the Prophet.

Opposite: Dome of the Rock, Jerusalem.
Page 32 above: The facade of Dome of the Rock;
Page 32 below: The Wailing Wall and Temple Mount, Jerusalem.
Page 33: Church of the Holy Sepulchre, Jerusalem.

THE WONDER OF IT

Jerusalem is a city where cultures clash, histories entwine and spirituality is all around. The Holy City is sacred to three religions, each of which has battled for its possession. For the Jews, it is the location of their holiest site, and the ancestral and spiritual home of the Jewish people. For Christians, it is the site of Christ's crucifixion and resurrection. And for Muslims, it is where Muhammad travelled from Mecca to Jerusalem and ascended to heaven after praying at the Dome of the Rock, the third most sacred shrine of Islam.

IN SEARCH OF THE DEAD SEA SCROLLS

QUMRAN, ISRAEL

AN INTRIGUING DISCOVERY

Some unremarkable clay jars lay buried deep in various dusty caves in the desert for thousands of years, untouched and unnoticed. Until, that is, a Bedouin shepherd stumbled upon seven of them in 1947. Opening one up, he found scrolls of parchment and animal skin covered in writing, wrapped in crumbling folds of cloth. A dealer in antiquities bought the cache, which eventually led to fragments of the scrolls coming to the attention of American biblical scholar and archaeologist John C Trever. He recognized their importance and value and announced their discovery to the world.

At first, the Bedouin kept the location of the scrolls under wraps, but after a couple of years, the truth was out. The limestone caves were located near Qumran, Israel, about 1.5km (1 mile) from the northwestern shore of the Dead Sea. In 1952, French and American teams of archaeologists investigated further and found fragments of 800–900 manuscripts dating from 150 BCE to 70 CE. The scrolls were dated back to the time of Christ and told of a

religious community not dissimilar to the first Christians. Soon this was hailed as the greatest manuscript discovery of our times, and debate and controversy about their meaning and purpose started in earnest.

THE TALES THEY TELL

It is generally thought that the Scrolls were the library of a Jewish sect known as the Essenes. Life in their monastery, which was on a nearby plateau, was austere and ascetic: they wore plain linen loincloths, ate frugally, lived quietly and spent much of their time studying scriptures. They believed that they were the elect and would be the sole survivors of an apocalypse. Like the early Christians, the Essenes eschewed material goods. They also performed cleansing rituals similar to those of Christian baptisms.

The Dead Sea Scrolls include fragments from every book of the Old Testament, except for the Book of Esther (which still may be found), prayers, psalms, commentaries and material relating to Judgement Day. The only complete book of the Hebrew Bible among the scrolls is

Isaiah, making it the earliest Old Testament manuscript in existence. They are mostly written in Hebrew, although some are in Aramaic (the language of the Jews of Palestine at that time) and a few are written in Greek.

Of all the scrolls, the Copper Scroll is the most tantalizing. Unlike the others, which are written in ink on parchment or leather, the Copper Scroll has been chiselled onto metal sheets. It indicates 64 underground places around Israel where valuable items have been buried. None of these has been discovered, but the chances are they were sacked long ago, or never even existed.

The Dead Sea Scrolls are now housed in the Shrine of the Book in the grounds of the Israel Museum, in the holy city of Jerusalem.

Opposite: The Qumran caves where the Dead Sea Scrolls were discovered.

AD DEIR MONASTERY

PETRA, JORDAN

THE WONDER OF IT

The ruined rock city of Petra was lost until the 19th century, buried beneath the desert sand, kept secret by the local people. It is one of the most spectacular sites in the Middle East. Its massive carved facades glow soft pink as the sun sets, and glitter and flash when caught by the midday sun. At its heart is the monumental monastery of Ad Deir, reached by climbing nearly 800 steps.

A HAND-CARVED CITY

Petra is approached through a 1.2-km (¾-mile) dark, narrow gorge called the Siq, whose sheer walls soar overhead, almost touching. At the end stands a building known as Al-Khazneh, or The Treasury – actually the tomb of royalty (probably Nabataean King Aretas IV) – with a magnificent facade carved out of pink sandstone. It is a mighty entrance to an incredible place. The road winds on down a valley to a series of sacred buildings, past grottos, stone benches and tombs, and three places of worship: the Temple of Dhu-Shara, the Temple of the Winged Lions and, high above them all, the Ad Deir Monastery.

Like other buildings at Petra, the monastery is cut from soft pink sandstone. It is massive in scale – 48m (157ft) high and 50m (164ft) wide – and was constructed in 3 BCE, probably as a tomb for the Nabataean king Obodas. A nearby inscription reads: "The symposium of Obodas, the god." (Obodas was probably deified posthumously.) From up here, there are views of the surrounding valleys, gorges and semi-arid landscape, across which merchants travelled to do trade at this once-powerful place.

A FRAGILE PLACE

One of the many astonishing things about the city of Petra is that the temples and tombs – hundreds of them – were carved by hand out of the rock face. This was possible because the rock – sandstone – is so soft; it can easily be chipped away and even crumbled in the hand. Fortunately, Jordan has virtually no rain, and carvings are set deep into the cliff, so the monuments have withstood erosion from wind. The sandstone is also why Petra is called "The Rose City": the rocks change colour during the day, glowing an especially lovely reddish pink at sunset and sunrise. Try to arrive early when the colour is at its most spectacular and the crowds have yet to arrive.

Opposite: The Ad Deir Monastery is loveliest at sunrise and sunset when it glows reddish pink.

PIR-E SABZ (CHAK-CHAK)

YAZD, IRAN

THE WONDER OF IT

A flame constantly burns in this shallow cave perched high on a cliff in the Iranian desert. Sacred to the people of the Zoroastrian faith, it is an important pilgrimage site and place of ritual.

> *Chak-chak* is the sound water makes as it falls, and gives the cave its alternative name.

FIRE AT ITS HEART

Every year, from 14 to 18 June, thousands of Zoroastrians from all over the world climb 420 steps in the searing heat to the fire temple at Pir-e Sabz. To them, this sacred grotto clinging to the side of a steep cliff-like mountain in central Iran, is an important *pir* (pilgrimage site) and place of ritual.

Dedicated to Princess Nikbanou, the grotto sits behind two large bronze doors. In the centre, a keeper tends to the sacred flame which burns constantly, darkening the walls with soot. Water drips steadily from a spring in the rock walls known as Aab-e Hayat (water of life); the water pools on the floor supporting an ancient tree and a weeping willow (*sabz* means greenery).

FIRE RITUALS

Zoroastrians are often mistakenly identified as fire worshippers because their rituals involve fire and because it is present in their temples. Although they give thanks for the warmth and light that fire brings, they see it rather as an embodiment of God, not a god in its own right, and, along with water, as an agent of purity. Its clean white ash is used for purification ceremonies. Before entering a fire temple, shoes are removed, men don white caps and women wrap themselves in white scarves. Priests wear veils to prevent their breath contaminating the purity of the sacred flame.

Right: The Zoroastrian temple of Pir-e Sabz (Chak Chak).

KNOW A THING OR TWO ABOUT: ZOROASTRIANISM

Yazd is the historic capital of Zoroastrianism, a religion founded in about 600 BCE by the Persian prophet Zoroaster. He believed he had seen visions of a benevolent God he called Ahura Mazda, who is in constant battle with the evil demon Angra Mainyu. This duality is the core of Zoroastrian belief. Fire is venerated as the element of Ahura Mazda. Centuries of persecution have forced Zoroastrians to flee, and their numbers have much diminished over the years.

MYTHS & MAGIC: THE PRINCESS & THE SHRINE

The shrine at Pir-e Sabz is dedicated to Princess Nikbanou, the second daughter of King Yazdegerd III. Yazdegerd III ruled over the Sassanian Empire, the last pre-Islamic empire before the Muslim conquest. During the invasion by the Arab army in 640 CE, Yazdegerd was captured, but Nikbanou sheltered in a cave where she prayed for protection. The water that drips from the cave walls is said to be the princess's tears of grief, and the maidenhair fern that grows there a symbol of her hair.

ASIA

The countries of the Far East are drenched in spirituality and mysticism. Spirits reside in mountains, forests, hot springs and caves. The dead and the dying are honoured in rituals at temples and in rivers. Shrines, sanctuaries and islands are destinations for Hindu, Buddhist and Shinto pilgrims. It is a world of elaborate temples and sacred landscapes, rich in meaning and deep in faith.

BALI

Spirituality is everywhere on the Indonesian island of Bali. Its dramatic mountains, coral reefs, waterfalls, volcanic-sand beaches, lakes and jungly interior are respected and often worshipped by its inhabitants, the majority of whom are Hindu. Balinese Hinduism is a mixture of animism and Buddhism and is governed by a belief that the world is composed of opposing forces – whether they be good and evil, order and disorder, or gods and demons – that need to be balanced. The aim is to achieve enlightenment by practising karma and so escape the endless cycle of death and rebirth. It is a demanding faith, which requires its followers to conduct regular and often elaborate rituals. Countless ceremonies take place to honour everything from trees and animals to birth and cremation.

Even in the most popular tourist spots, a *pura* (temple) is only a few steps away. There are around 20,000 on Bali, more than there are homes, and they are at the heart of every *banjar* (neighbourhood), each of which is required to have three. Surrounded by high stone walls and without roofs (to allow easy access for the gods) they contain courtyards, shrines and altars, and can look confusing to the uninitiated. At the top of the village is the holiest *pura,* the *pura puseh,* dedicated to the community's founders. At the centre is the *pura desa,* a place for everyday spiritual activities, and at the end of the village is the *pura dalem,* the temple of the dead, where ancestors are remembered.

The Balinese consider the three mountains at the island's heart to be the realm of deities: the sea to be inhabited by demons and giants; the valleys in between occupied by humans. The highest and holiest mountain of the three is Gunung Agung, which is also an active volcano, and is where Bali's most sacred "mother" temple, Besakih, is found. Besakih is one of nine directional temples located on mountains, cliffs and lakes, to protect the island and its people. The other two mountains, Gunung Batur and Gunung Batukaru, also hold great spiritual power.

All temples, houses and villages are aligned in relation to the landscape that surrounds them: the holiest direction *(kaja)* looks towards the mountains, and upstream. The downstream direction *(kelod)* is closest to the sea

Above: A statute adorned with offerings in Ubud.
Opposite: Sunrise over paddy fields, with active volcano Gunung Agung in the distance.

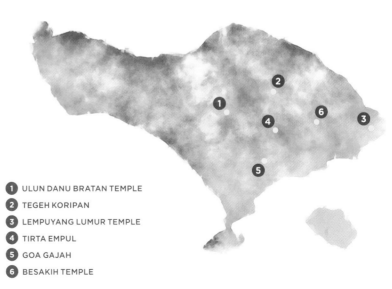

1 ULUN DANU BRATAN TEMPLE
2 TEGEH KORIPAN
3 LEMPUYANG LUMUR TEMPLE
4 TIRTA EMPUL
5 GOA GAJAH
6 BESAKIH TEMPLE

(where the demons live) and is therefore impure. On the anniversary of each temple's creation they become the focus of a loud and colourful festival. Purification is another important element of Balinese Hinduism, and temples such as Tirta Empul, in Tampaksiring, are centred around holy springs, pools and gushing spouts, where visitors can bathe and participate in cleansing rituals.

During the Balinese New Year celebration in March, electricity is switched off over the entire island, flights are cancelled, and everyone stays at home in the dark to encourage bad spirits to fly over Bali without stopping. It is a quiet, peaceful time when the stars appear to shine brighter in the sky, and is symbolic of the island's reverential approach to the sacred.

LAOTIAN SPIRIT CULT

Although Laos is a Buddhist country, the practice of *phi* (spirit) worship is ever-present. This belief, which pre-dates Buddhism, recognizes that *phi* are everywhere; in trees, animals, buildings and people. Some *phi* are good, some are bad and some are plain mischievous. To placate the *phi* and keep them happy, miniature spirit houses are built outside homes and temples. Offerings of food and incense are placed inside them to ensure that the *phi* will not make trouble for the inhabitants.

THE WONDER OF IT: SACRED HIGHLIGHTS

BESAKIH TEMPLE: Bali's biggest and holiest temple is reached by climbing steps 1,000m (3,300ft) up the slopes of Mount Agung. Best visited in early morning or evening when the spirit of the place is easier to hear. This is a complex of 86 temples, including the sacred Pura Penatran Agung, and is a Hindu pilgrimage.

GOA GAJAH, UBUD (THE ELEPHANT CAVE): Enter the grimacing mouth gateway into a dark cave occupied by statues of idols wrapped in cloths. Outside are bathing pools, fountains and carvings.

LEMPUYANG LUHUR TEMPLE: Accessible only on foot up 1,700 steps, this is one of the oldest temples in Bali. At the summit, a priest blesses pilgrims with a sprinkling of holy water.

TIRTA EMPUL, TAMPAKSIRING: Purification rites are an essential element of Balinese Hinduism, and this water temple with its holy springs is the place to do it.

GITGIT WATERFALL: Two cascades of water fall into a rocky pool 40m (131ft) below. A place for spiritual healing and purification.

THE POSES OF BUDDHA
& THE POWER OF 108

KNOW A THING OR TWO ABOUT: BUDDHA POSES

The various types of Buddha statues can be identified by their gestures, especially their hand gestures (*mudra*), each of which conveys a different spiritual meaning. The following are the most common:

1 **BHUMISPARSHA MUDRA:** Buddha is seated with legs in lotus position. His left hand is in his lap, palm facing upwards, and his right hand rests on his knee, pointing towards the earth. *Bhumisparsha* means "touching the earth" or "calling the earth to witness" and represents the moment when Buddha reached enlightenment under the Bodhi tree.

2 **DHYANA MUDRA:** Buddha is seated in lotus position with both hands in his lap. His thumbs touch, forming a triangle, and his eyes are closed or semi-closed in an attitude of focused concentration. This represents Buddha in meditation. Offerings are sometimes placed in his hands.

3 **ABHAYA MUDRA:** Buddha is seated in lotus position (and sometimes standing) with his right hand raised, palm facing out and fingers pointing up. His left hand is in his lap (or by his side). This represents Buddha immediately after achieving enlightenment and signifies fearlessness and courage.

4 **VARADA MUDRA:** Buddha is seated in lotus position with his right hand extended towards the earth, with the palm facing outwards. His left hand is in his lap facing upwards. The five extended fingers represent the five perfections: generosity, morality, patience, effort and concentration.

5 **RECLINING BUDDHA:** Buddha is lying down on his right side; his head rests on a cushion or is supported by his right hand. This represent Buddha's last moments of life on Earth, before he entered *parinirvana* – death following nirvana.

THE POWER OF 108

Of all numbers, 108 is the most sacred for Buddhists. Woven into many faiths and beliefs for centuries, it occurs in different teachings and as a measurement used in the construction of sacred buildings. Why this is the case is open to interpretation: it could be some form of divine mathematics perhaps, or an association with the workings of the human body, or maybe it has an astrological connection.

   Whatever the reason, it is an important number because:

• In **Buddhism** there are 108 mortal desires (or delusions). Buddhist prayer beads (*malas*) number 108 accordingly. Many Buddhist temples have 108 steps representing the 108 steps to enlightenment.

• In **Hinduism** deities have 108 names. India is also said to have 108 sacred sites.

• In **Jainism** there are 108 virtues.

• In some forms of **tai chi** there are 108 moves.

• At **Zen Buddhist** temples in Japan, a bell is chimed 108 times at the end of the year, as a reminder of the 108 earthly temptations that must be overcome to reach nirvana.

• In **yoga**, pranayama (a breathing exercise) is often completed in cycles of 108. Sun salutations are frequently performed in rounds of 12 postures, totalling 108.

"Be where you are, otherwise you will miss your life."
Buddha

Opposite: A Buddha statue in the lotus position, one of the more common Buddha poses, in Sukothai, Thailand.

NGŪ HÀNH SO'N

DA NANG, VIETNAM

MARBLE MOUNTAINS

Ngū Hành So'n means "five-element mountain". Each of the five limestone mountains that rise 8km (5 miles) south of the coastal city of Da Nang represents a different element. Thuy So'n is water, Moc So'n is wood or plants, Hoa So'n is fire, Kim So'n is metal or gold and Tho So'n is earth.

Tho So'n (earth): The largest mountain is a place of pilgrimage – several of its caves contain Buddhist statues and there are remains of temples scattered about.

Thuy So'n (water): This is the most visited mountain. It has many shrines and pagodas either on its slopes or inside caves. The 17th-century Tam Thai Pagoda is reached by climbing 156 stone steps along the spine of the mountain. A climb down stone steps to Huyen Khong ("Heavenly Light") cave leads to a monumental statue of the Buddha, and then, further in, the 19th-century Trang Nghiēm Tu Temple, where three goddesses representing morality, wisdom and loyalty are worshipped.

Kim So'n (metal or gold): Tucked away in the cliffs on this mountain is the Quan Am cavern, which houses a large female *bodhisattva* statue (see page 49), a pool of pure, clear water, and a stalactite that rings like a bell when tapped.

Moc So'n (wood or plants): Moc So'n has been denuded of much of its vegetation and has been heavily quarried – best to climb the other mountains instead.

Hoa So'n (fire): This is actually two mountains connected by a natural rock road. Two ancient pagodas – Linh So'n Pagoda (and Huyen Vi cave) and Pho Da So'n Pagoda (and cave) – perch on the craggy mountain slopes, as do the remains of several Cham temples.

The best time of year to climb the mountains is from June to August, because the steps that lead to the summits get wet and slippery during the stormy season (September to November). Early in the morning, when there are fewer people and the air is still cool, is the ideal time of day.

HELL CAVE

Near Thuy So'n, the Am Phu Cave, or "Hell Cave", is a re-creation of Buddhist hell, with freaky-looking rock formations populated with fanged demons and nippy crocodiles illuminated by shafts of light. Mere mortals must pass through this dark, dank and devilish world before they ascend a steep stone staircase to the outside, where heaven awaits. The 302m- (991ft-) long cave, which reaches heights of 50m (164ft), is a vivid diorama illustrating the principle of karma: everything we do has consequences; bad behaviour results in a suitable comeuppance.

Opposite: A Buddhist temple and place of pilgrimage in a cave, Da Nang.

ANGKOR WAT

SIEM REAP, CAMBODIA

THE WONDER OF IT

Consumed by jungle for centuries, this is a spectacular cityscape of elaborate carved temples, giant Buddaha heads and waterways, its most outstanding features being Angkor Wat, a temple with five central towers dedicated to Vishnu; Angkor Thom, a walled complex containing the Buddhist Bayon Temple; and Ta Prohm, a crumbling temple locked in the jungle's clinch.

A LOST TEMPLE

In 1860, French naturalist Henri Mouhot, who had heard of the ruined city of Angkor, made his way through the jungle to find it. What he discovered was a massive temple complex smothered by creepers, tree roots and vines. Built between the 12th and 15th centuries by a succession of Khmer emperors, it sprawled over 1,000 sq m (10,800 sq ft) and comprised a walled city surrounded by a multitude of temples. Mouhot chronicled his discoveries in journals, comparing the site to the Great Pyramids of Egypt. Once word was out, archaeologists and historians followed in his footsteps, excited by, and trying to make sense of, this fantastical place.

Angkor Wat was built by the Khmer King Suryavarman II, a great innovator in the worlds of art and architecture. Created to represent the Hindu mountain Meru, home of the gods, the temple was also a celebration of Suryavarman II's divinity (Khmer rulers were regarded as god-kings) and was his funerary monument. Facing west, towards the land of the dead, it rises in tiers from terraces adorned with galleries and pavilions to a pyramid formed by the five towers. Its walls are embellished with carvings of almost 2,000 *aspara* (celestial dancing nymphs) and long stretches of reliefs depicting Hindu legends and scenes.

One hundred years later, the last great Khmer king, Jayavarman VII, built Angkor Thom, a new walled city with a multi-faceted, multi-towered temple at its heart. Now called the Bayon Temple, it mixed Hindu and Buddhist images, most famously the 216 smiling stone faces of Avalokiteshvara, a Buddhist *bodhisattva* (an enlightened being destined eventually to become a buddha, see below) who embodies compassion. The largest of these adorn the four sides of each temple tower, each facing a different cardinal point. Nearby are other complexes protected by moats once full of crocodiles and with gateways big enough to allow elephants to pass.

It can get very crowded at peak time, so it's best to visit just after sunrise to enjoy the peace that settles over this amazing place.

Opposite: The temple of Angkor Wat was dedicated to the Hindu god Vishnu.

KNOW A THING OR TWO ABOUT BODHISATTVAS

In Buddhism, and Mahayana Buddhism in particular, *Bodhisattvas* are holy people who forego personal nirvana to help others achieve enlightenment. They make a vow not to enter nirvana until all beings can enter together.

SRI PADA (ADAM'S PEAK)

RATNAPURA, SRI LANKA

THE WONDER OF IT

Looking unlike any mountain nearby, this tall, conical peak is a worthy pilgrimage destination. A large rock formation near the summit – claimed by different religions to be a sacred footprint – draws thousands annually to clamber up its steep sides.

FOLLOWING A FOOTPRINT

It can get crowded on the path to the summit of Adam's Peak. Ascent is limited to December–May, with April being the most popular month for pilgrims. At other times, heavy rain, wind and thick mist make ascent difficult and pointless. To get there, most people take a train to Hatton, then a taxi, bus or tuk-tuk to the nearest town of Dalhousie to stay overnight, before setting off early in the morning (around 3am) to reach the top at sunrise. The route, which is lit and decked with flags, goes up crumbling steep stone steps, past a Peace Pagoda at the halfway point, and shops selling refreshments. It is

a tough climb, but the rewards are worth it: at sunrise the mountain casts a triangular shadow over the surrounding landscape, and there are views as far as the Indian Ocean.

True pilgrims also make the climb to visit the shrine in the temple at the summit and to venerate the Sri Pada (sacred footprint), a 1.8-m (6-ft) indentation in the rock, sheltered under a tiny gold pavilion and guarded by monks. Some collect the water that pools there, considering it holy. The mountain has been a place of pilgrimage for more than 1,000 years, principally for Buddhists who believe the sacred footprint to have been created by Buddha. Other religions also claim it. In Hindu tradition, it's thought to be the *padam* (foot) of Shiva or of Hanuman. Some Muslim traditions say it was here that Prophet Adam first stepped when cast out of heaven: he stood on one foot until his sins were forgiven (hence the mountain's English name). And some Portuguese Christians believe it to be the footprint of St Thomas.

Right: Sri Pada, a place of pilgrimage for more than a thousand years.

MIYAJIMA

HATSUKAICHI, JAPAN

THE WONDER OF IT

The red *torii* (gateway) to the island of Itsukushima – more commonly referred to as Miyajima (temple island) – was built over water to allow pilgrims to visit without treading on the island's sacred ground. The entire island is a holy landscape for followers of Shintoism and Buddhism, from its mountain peak to its many temples and shrines.

A SACRED LANDSCAPE

The gateway to Miyajima's Itsukushima Temple is an appropriate introduction to this sacred island. At high tide, its two red pillars topped by a cross beam appear to float above the water of the Seto Inland Sea. Gateways (*torii*) like this are a feature of Shinto shrines – there is always at least one, sometimes several, outside each. In this case, the island was considered so sacred that no commoner was permitted to set foot on it. Arrival was by boat through the *torii*, and entrance to the shrine was only permitted by walking over boardwalks suspended above the ground. No burials were allowed on the island and pregnant women had to leave to give birth elsewhere, to preserve its purity.

Now, of course, the island is one of Japan's most photographed attractions, with many visitors arriving daily. To get there, catch a train from Hiroshima station to Miyajimaguchi, then catch a ferry to Miyajima, a ten-minute journey. It is still possible, however, to appreciate the spiritual sanctity of this place, which continues to be a foremost sanctuary for followers of Shintoism and Buddhism.

The Itsukushima Temple, which has been on this site since the 6th century (although the present buildings date from the 13th century), is an important Shinto place of worship. Its 17 buildings and two shrine complexes include a prayer hall, a main hall and a floating Noh (or *nō*) theatre stage, which is still used for performances of this classical Japanese dance-drama form. In the tradition of Japanese Shinto architecture, a mountain or natural object is the focus of worship, and it is important that the built structure is in harmony with it and its surroundings. Itsukushima's position on the sea, with Mount Misen behind, conforms to this and is recognized as a Japanese standard of beauty. The shrine itself is dedicated to three female Shinto deities, the *sanjoshin*, who are goddesses of seas and storms.

Mount Misen, the island's tallest peak, is itself sacred, not just for followers of Shintoism, but also for Shingon Buddhists – at its foot is the Daishō-in Temple where Kūkai Daishi, the founder of the cult, meditated for 100 days. A flame that he lit 1,200 years ago still burns.

A path from the temple up stone steps is lined with wheels on which *sutra* (Buddhist scriptures) are written. Pilgrims spin them as they pass – an act thought to be as valuable as reading the words. The path leads to the summit of the mountain, 530m (1,740ft) high, a lovely walk in the spring when the cherry blossom is out, and in autumn when the leaves change colour. From the top, there are views of forests, ocean and islands.

Opposite: The torii gateway at Miyajima appears to float above the water.

KNOW A THING OR TWO ABOUT: SHINTOISM

Shinto, or Shintoism, is an indigenous Japanese religion that venerates nature. It is based on the belief that spirits (*kami*) are present in mountains, trees, rocks, springs and other natural features. Humans become *kami* after they die and are revered by their families as ancestral *kami*.

The sun goddess Amaterasu is considered Shinto's most important *kami* and is ruler of the *kami* domain. All major Shinto shrines are found in surroundings of great natural beauty. The religion has no founder, dogma or scriptures but is rooted in Japanese myth and traditions.

SHIKOKU ISLAND

JAPAN

THE WONDER OF IT

The trail around the island of Shikoku strings 88 temples together in a circular pilgrimage that marries the beautiful landscape with Buddhist teachings.

A SPIRITUAL JOURNEY

The best way to understand a landscape is to walk through it, and nowhere is this more true than on the Japanese island of Shikoku. The fastest way to reach Shikoku is by bus through Awaji Island. Alternatively catch a ferry from Kobe or Hiroshima, which takes about 2.5 hours. A well-marked 1,200-km (750-mile) trail takes pilgrims to forests and waterfalls, up mountains, across streams, into temples, past shrines and through circular "moon gates". This pilgrimage route is thought to owe its inception to a monk called Kūkai Daishi (774–835), who did much to popularize Buddhism, and his presence and sacred traces are acknowledged and felt all along the path.

The pilgrimage was originally intended for monks, but by the 17th century everyone was invited to walk the route. Modern Buddhist pilgrims, called *henro*, are recognizable by their white clothes. Some also wear wide-brimmed conical hats and carry *kongo-zue* (walking sticks). The words *dōgyō ninin* ("two travelling together") are frequently written on their hats or jackets and refer to the constant spiritual presence of Kūkai, who is seen as a guardian and guide.

The journey begins at Ryōzenji Temple in Tokushima prefecture (Shikoku has four prefectures), then circles the island, stopping at 88 temples along the way. Alms (*osettai*) – coins, incense – are given at each one. Every temple has its own associations: Kōnomineji (temple 27), is known for its healing waters; Uapenji (66) has an aubergine-shaped seat that is said to grant wishes; Zentsūji (75) has an annual ceremony to celebrate the arrival of a noodle dish from China. The final temple, Okuboji (88), is in Kagawa prefecture.

The journey through the four prefectures is likened to a symbolic path to enlightenment: temples 1–23 represent awakening; 24–39 austerity and discipline; 40–65

attaining enlightenment; and 66–88 entering nirvana. *Henro* (pilgrims) chant the heart *sutra* at each temple. To complete the entire walk takes about 40 days, although some *henro* choose to walk one section only, or travel part of it by bus or train.

This is a spiritual journey and *henro* leave behind daily concerns to concentrate on the path and its potential for personal growth. It is increasingly attracting pilgrims from other countries, and guesthouses catering for them have sprung up along the route. Unlike other linear pilgrimage routes, such as El Camino de Santiago, it is satisfyingly circular. This doesn't make it any easier, however: there are mountains to climb and much distance to walk, but overcoming difficulties is one of the points of pilgrimage, after all.

"Form is no different to emptiness, emptiness no different to form. That which is form is emptiness, that which is emptiness, form. Sensations, perceptions, impressions, and consciousness are also like this."
Extract from *The Heart Sutra*:

Opposite: Konsenji Temple, the third on the Shikoku pilgrimage.

MOUNT HAKUSAN, MOUNT TATEYAMA & MOUNT FUJI

MOUNT HAKUSAN

This range of snowcapped mountains in Japan is known to followers of Hakusan Shinkō (who worship mountain *kami*, or nature spirits) as a "mountain realm inhabited by *kami*". It is the most important and ancient site of *sangaku shūkyō* (mountain worship), and has been a place of pilgrimage since the 8th century.

After the founder of Shugendō Buddhism climbed the mountain to meditate, it also became a training site for monks to teach them the ascetic practices associated with Shugendō. Shugendō followers are called *yamabushi*, which means "mountain priests". For a while, monks were the only people allowed to set foot on Hakusan, but as mountain worship and pilgrimage grew in popularity, everyone was welcome.

Two main trails lead to the highest, at 2,702m (8,865ft), and most sacred peak, Gozenpō (also called Gozengamine) – the more popular trail takes eight to ten hours. A good place to start (and end for a satisfying muscle-easing soak) is the Shiramine Onsen (a small hot spring and a large public bath). The ascent ends at a Shinto shrine on the summit: many people aim to get there for sunrise.

MOUNT TATEYAMA

This sacred mountain in Japan is actually a ridge comprising three peaks: Onanji, the highest, at 3,015m (9,892ft); Oyama; and Fujinooritate. A mountain-worship shrine is at the summit of Onanji (alongside a shop selling souvenirs), and climbers receive a blessing and a cup of warm sake from a priest on arrival... for a fee!

The mountain landscape here is varied and beautiful. Wild flowers carpet the slopes in summer. A still, volcanic lake (Mikurigaike) mirrors the bright blue sky. A forest of beech trees that are 200–300 years old softens the mountain's jagged outline, and sulphur springs provides water for *onsen* (hot springs) baths. Little wonder, then, that Tateyama means "outstanding mountain".

As a result, it can get very crowded at the peak climbing period (April–November), so it's best to arrive early. You'll be rewarded at the summit (on a clear day) with views of Shōmyō Falls – the tallest waterfall in Japan – across the valley and Mount Fuji in the distance. There are a variety of well-marked trails to guide you safely up the mountain's sacred slopes.

MOUNT FUJI

Mount Fuji, Japan is one of the world's most recognizable, and most sacred, mountains. It was first considered sacred by the Ainu (the indigenous people of Japan) and is named after their fire goddess Fuchi. For Shintoists, it is the home of Sengen-Sama, goddess of blossoms, who is said to live in a luminous cloud within the mountain's crater and preside over a healing stream on its southern side. Her shrine, most often snow-covered, is at the top of the mountain. Shugendō Buddhists see it as a gateway to another world and too holy to be trod upon lightly.

Sacred Japanese mountains, Tateyana (left) and Fuji (right) should be trod upon lightly.

JAPANESE ONSEN

THE NATURAL SOUL SOOTHER

In Japan, you are never far from a hot spring. It is estimated that there are more than 3,000 *onsen* (hot springs) in Japan, where they are an essential part of daily life.

Traditionally, *onsen* were sacred places of healing where ailments could be eased. Samurai warriors were said to head to one after a battle to heal their wounds.

Each spring has different benefits, depending on the mineral composition of the water. Iron-rich water soothes painful joints; sulphur manages blood pressure and prevents hardening of the arteries; hydrogen carbonate makes the skin smooth.

These days, the mental as well as physical benefits of *onsen* are increasingly recognized. Shintoism has always acknowledged the power of immersion in water as an aid to spiritual purification. Its followers practise *misogi* – standing beneath a waterfall for a thorough drenching. *Onsen* offer a gentler approach: an hour or two bathing in an outdoor pool – called *rotenburo*, or "bathing amid the dew under the open sky" – is considered to have the power to soothe the soul. Natural *onsen* can be found beneath waterfalls, beside rivers or on the edge of forests. Often they are part of a *ryokan* (traditional hot spring inn) which offers accommodation as well as the whole *onsen* experience.

Japanese healing hot springs: Kusuatsu onsen (above); the lake at Jigoku Numa (opposite, above); Awanoyu (opposite below).

THE RITUAL OF THE ONSEN

A visit to an *onsen* is for cleansing the soul and healing the body. It's a meditative process that gives you time to renew, revive and reconnect with yourself inside and out. To get the most out of the experience, there are certain procedures to follow:

1   Embrace nudity. Getting naked is mandatory at most *onsen*. Some permit swimsuits, but they are rare.

2   Everyone showers thoroughly before entering. Shower stations flank entrances and comprise a low wooden stool and a mounted shower hose and bucket made from Japanese cypress (*hinoki*). Bathers soap their entire bodies and rinse with the hand shower while sitting on the stool. It is important not to pollute the *onsen*, to keep the water as pure as possible.

3   Now clean, you can enter the spring. Depending on the *onsen*, there is a choice of places to immerse yourself, some outdoors, some indoors.

4   Once in the geothermal waters, there is nothing to do but bob about and enjoy the moment. If the temperature gets too hot, hop out and sit on a rock to cool off.

LUMBINI

RUPANDEHI, NEPAL

THE WONDER OF IT

The birthplace of Buddha draws pilgrims from all around the world. It is a place to wander around, marvel and reflect. It is also a place of healing and serenity.

FROM HUMBLE VILLAGE TO CITY OF TEMPLES

It was at Lumbini, roughly 2,500 years ago, that an Indian queen, Maya Devi, "walked 20 paces, grabbed the branch of a tree and faced to the east" before giving birth to her son, Siddhartha Gautama, who later became Buddha, the "Awakened One". The place of his birth is marked by a terracotta slab in the Maya Devi Temple, which is devoted to his mother, and is a place of pilgrimage for Buddhists from all over the world.

After Buddha's death, the village of Lumbini was transformed into a religious community. *Stupas* (dome-shaped buildings to house Buddhist relics) and prayer halls were built around the place of Buddha's birth,

and pilgrims started to arrive. One of these was the Emperor Ashoka, an evangelist for Buddhism, who called by in the 3rd century BCE and left behind a stone pillar to mark the occasion. As Hinduism spread and Buddhism receded, the city and its buildings were abandoned. The Ashoka Pillar was struck by lightning. Lumbini fell into ruin. It would have been lost if it hadn't been for a local governor and a German archaeologist who unearthed the Ashoka Pillar in 1896. Lumbini was back in the spotlight, and its rebirth as a major Buddhist pilgrimage site began.

The Maya Devi Temple was rebuilt on the site of previous temples dating back to the 3rd century BCE. Around it is a network of canals, a sacred pool (the Puskami, where Maya Devi took a ritual dip before Buddha's birth), gardens and bridges that take you from *stupa* to temple to ancient ruin. As you walk, you pass monks sitting beneath Bodhi trees (sacred fig trees) meditating like Buddha once did, as prayer flags flutter overhead.

Maya Devi is the main temple at Lumbini, but there are many others. Sitting side by side in the Monastic Zone (a large area bordering Lumbini in which only monasteries

may be built), each temple represents Buddhism as it is architecturally interpreted by different countries. There is the Japanese World Peace Pagoda, a brilliant white *stupa* with a golden Buddha in the posture of his birth at its heart. The Zhong Hua Chinese Buddhist Monastery is built in an elegant pagoda style with two tiers of red tile roofs. The massive Korean Buddhist Temple is intricately painted and lavishly decorated. And the Cambodian Monastery has triple towers reminiscent of the five towers at Angkor Wat (see pages 48–9). There are plenty more, and new temples continue to be built. It is still a peaceful place to wander and reflect, to find a quiet spot beneath a tree, beside a pool or in one of the temples.

Opposite: Buddhist prayer flags in Lumbini.

THE LIFE OF BUDDHA

• Born Siddhartha Gautama in Lumbini, Nepal, into a royal family. Dates vary, but it could have been as early as 624 BCE.

• As a prince, and a member of the warrior caste, he lives a life of luxury and privilege and is expected to become a ruler. He is taught combat skills such as archery and lives a protected life.

• Aged 29, he finally ventures from the palace and encounters people in the grip of suffering and pain. He realizes that old age, sickness and death come to everyone.

• Meeting a monk deep in meditation, he realizes that the truth he seeks is to be found within.

• He secretly leaves the palace and sets off into the forest, spending six years listening to wise people and learning meditation.

• Having spent several days and nights meditating at Bodh Gaya beneath a Bodhi tree (see pages 102–103), he reaches enlightenment. He is one week away from his 35th birthday. He becomes Buddha, the Awakened One.

• He walks around northern India sharing his wisdom and teachings for 45 years until his death (or release from mortal pain).

THE MONASTERIES OF LADAKH
NORTHERN INDIA

LOST KINGDOM

Wild, barren, mountainous and relatively unvisited, Ladakh in northern India feels like a lost, magical kingdom. Multistorey *gompas* (monasteries) perch on top of rocky outcrops surrounded by whitewashed *stupa*, and prayer flags flutter in the breeze. The sound of monks chanting and the clamour of cymbals and drums being struck are commonplace: Tibetan Buddhism is very much alive here.

Most monasteries are open to visitors, and although some take a certain amount of determination to reach, their distinctive architecture and colourful interiors filled with glittering *Bodhisattva* statues (see page 49) and wall paintings make the journey worthwhile.

Leh, the capital of Ladakh, is a good base from which to explore local monasteries.

SIX MONASTERIES TO VISIT

1 **HEMIS:** Located in a valley rather than on a mountaintop, Hemis is the most visited *gompa* in Ladakh. About 150 *lamas* (Buddhist monks) of the Drukpa lineage live in this series of temple buildings, which contain the cave where Tantric master Gyalwang Gotsang (1189–1258) meditated.

2 **SHEY:** On a rocky perch beside a ruined palace, Shey houses a 12m- (40ft-) high statue of Buddha. Permission is needed to visit the monastery as it's occupied by a single *lama* and is not always open.

3 **THIKSE:** On a mountaintop 3,600m (11,800ft) up sits this 12-storey monastery, home to 500 Gelug Tibetan Buddhist monks. Its sacred treasures include a 15m- (49ft-) high statue of Maitreya Buddha seated in the lotus position, as well as a collection of precious texts, statues and *thangkas* (painting or appliqué on cotton or silk).

4 **LAMAYURU:** One of the main monasteries of the Drikung Kagyu lineage of Buddhism, Lamayuru is also one of the oldest and largest, and houses 150 monks.

5 **ALCHI:** This is the oldest monastery in Ladakh and has many *thangkas* and three major shrines, all elaborately decorated.

6 **DISKIT:** A Gelug Tibetan Buddhist monastery in a beautiful and serene setting in the Nubra Valley. Opposite is the mighty Maitreya Buddha which took six years to build before its inauguration by the Dalai Lama in 2010.

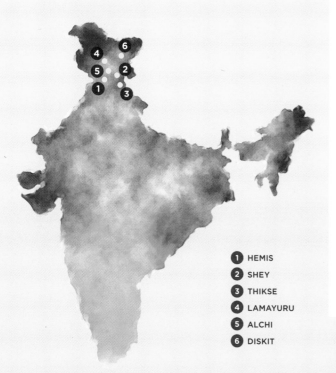

1 HEMIS
2 SHEY
3 THIKSE
4 LAMAYURU
5 ALCHI
6 DISKIT

Opposite: Maitreya Buddha near Diskit Monastery, Ladakh.

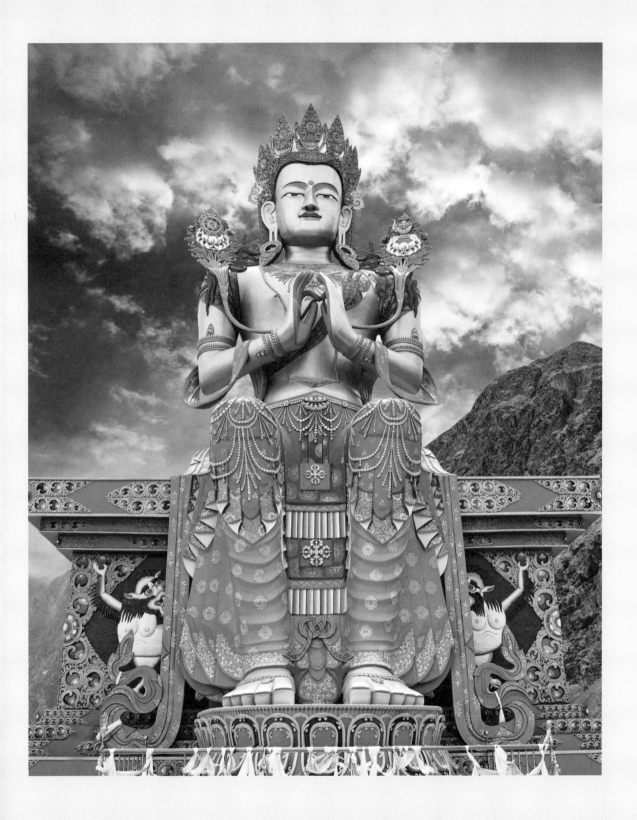

MONASTIC FESTIVALS

A visit to a Ladakh monastery during festival season is an immersive, sensory experience. Monks don elaborate, colourful silk costumes and wear masks representing deities and animals to perform *chams* (ritual dances). Their movements are performed in time to music played on *dungchen* (long horns), *silnyen* (cymbals), *dung* (conch shells) and *nga* (drums) and are watched by banks of local people and tourists.

FEBRUARY

Stok Guru Tsechu festival, Stok & Spituk Monasteries: Starting on the ninth day after Tibetan new year, this festival of prayers, dance, music and food is unusual because it is performed by laypeople, not monks. During the festivities, two local men appear as "oracles" and make forecasts for the new year.

Dosmoche, Likir & Diskit Monasteries: The last of the new year festivals is celebrated to bring safety and wellbeing to the people in the year ahead. *Cham* dances are performed by *lamas* to ward off evil and bring peace and happiness. They also make thread crosses to drive away evil spirits.

JUNE/JULY

Hemis Tse Chu, Hemis Monastery: A two-day festival of dancing performed by *lamas* (monks) wearing masks and costumes depicting the story of Padmasambhava, an 8th-century Buddhist master second in importance only to Buddha. Every 12 years, a 12m- (39ft-) long richly embroidered *tangkha* representing his life is brought out in celebration.

Yuru Kabgyat, Lamayuru Monastery: The teachings of Tibetan Buddhism are brought to life through traditional singing and dancing. Dances are dedicated to Yama (Lord of Death) and Padmasambhava who appear as costumed dancers.

Right: The 12m- (40ft-) high statue of Buddha at Shey.
Opposite above left: Dancing in costume at the Cham Dance Festival in Hemis.
Opposite above right: Lamayuru Monastery.
Opposite below: A white stupa near Shey Monastery, the Himalayas behind.

JULY/AUGUST

Tak Tok Festival, Tak Tok Monastery: Celebrated at the cave of the monastery, this is one of the main festivals in Ladakh and draws large numbers of people. Masked *lamas* in elaborate costumes perform *chams* based on the life of Padmasambhava. Green-masked demons roam among the crowd asking for contributions.

OCTOBER/NOVEMBER

Thikse Gustor, Thikse Monastery: This festival involves two days of chanting Buddhist *sutras* and giving offerings. On the second day, a dance is performed by traditional Black Hat dancers, culminating in a ceremony called Argham, or "killing", in which a sacrificial cake is destroyed and distributed among the people. This marks the end of the festival.

BHUTAN

The small, landlocked country of Bhutan in South Asia is a world apart. Its isolation has kept its culture intact and its natural environment unspoiled. Buddhism, the predominant religion, forms its identity. There are many *dzongs* (monasteries), some of which act as a stage for *tshechus* (dance festivals).

The north of the country is dominated by the Eastern Himalayas. Monasteries perch perilously on the sides of steep ravines, and switchback roads dart through forests and mountain passes. By law, at least 60 per cent of the country must remain forested for future generations; at the moment it is 70 per cent. The highest peak is Gangkhar Puensum, which is 7,570m (24,856ft) above sea level and has never been climbed: the people of Bhutan respect the sanctity of the mountain.

One of the reasons it preserves so much of its integrity is that it discourages visitors. Citizens of India, Bangladesh and the Maldives can enter freely, but all others have to pay a daily fee – an initiative devised to prevent low-cost tourism. Before arriving, visitors must sign up with a registered Bhutanese tour agency and pay a lump sum which covers the cost of accommodation, meals, a vehicle and driver, fuel and permits.

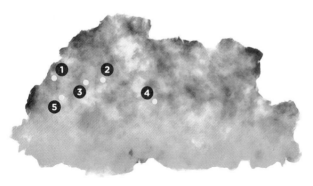

1. PARO TAKTSANG (TIGER'S NEST)
2. PUNAKHA DZONG
3. TASHICHHO DZONG, THIMPHU
4. TRONGSA DZONG
5. KYICHU LHAKHANG DZONG

SELECTED SACRED PLACES

PARO TAKTSANG (TIGER'S NEST): Miraculously perched on the side of a sheer cliff 900m (2,953ft) above the Paro Valley, this photogenic monastery requires a bit of legwork to get there – choose from one of three routes to ascend – but is totally worth it for the spectacular views.

PUNAKHA DZONG: Also known as "the palace of great happiness", this beautiful fortress sits on the confluence of two rivers: Pho Chhu (male) and Mo Chhu (female). It houses sacred Buddhist relics, murals depicting the life of Buddha and gilded statues. Every year it holds a five-day festival, Domche, which includes historical re-enactments and theatrical displays.

TASHICHHO DZONG, THIMPHU: This impressive monastery and fortress sits on the western bank of the Wangchhu River. The original structure was built in 1216 as a monastery. After being destroyed several times by fire and an earthquake, it was rebuilt in its present incarnation in 1968 using traditional methods – which means no nails or using any architectural plans. Once the seat of the Bhutanese government, it now houses the offices of the King and some other government departments, as well as a monastic quarter.

TRONGSA DZONG: Spectacularly situated over the river Mangde Chhu, this is the largest fortress in Bhutan. Within its walls are 25 temples, the most important of which are dedicated to tantric deities. Buildings seemingly tumble down the ridge and are connected by wide stone stairs, corridors and paved courtyards.

KYICHU LHAKHANG DZONG: One of Bhutan's oldest and most beautiful temples, it dates back to the 7th century, although its golden roof was added in 1839 by the then-governor of Paro.

Opposite above: Punakha Dzong.
Opposite below: Paro Taktsang (Tiger's Nest).

THE CHAR DHAM
UTTARAKHAND, INDIA

SPIRIT OF THE PEOPLE

Between April and November, the perilous mountain roads and stone footpaths of the Garhwal Himalayas throng with Hindu pilgrims. Every one is intent on reaching one, or all, of four sacred sites: Yamunotri, Gangotri, Kedarnath and Badrinath. Each of these temples marks the spiritual source of a sacred river: the Yamuna, the Ganges, the Mandakini and the Alaknanda. Together they form a holy pilgrimage known as the Char Dham ("four abodes").

In the past, travelling between the four abodes (temples) involved an arduous journey clambering up mountain paths – altitudes here are in excess of 3,000m (9,850ft). But better roads, transport links and accommodation mean that the circuit now takes 11–12 days accomplished both by foot and in various vehicles. The Char Dham begins at the source of the river Yamuna (the second holiest river in India after the Ganges), and travels through spectacular mountain scenery. A journey to one or two temples will immerse you in the faith and spirit of the people.

THE FOUR ABODES (DHAMS)

YAMUNOTRI: An hour and a half trek from the village of Janki Chatti takes pilgrims past waterfalls to a shrine containing the black marble statue of the goddess Yamuna. All around are hot springs – bathing here is thought to cleanse sins and protect from untimely and painful death. Some pilgrims boil rice and potatoes in the hot water to make a *prasad* (a religious offering that is later eaten).

GANGOTRI: This remote and modest temple is one of the holiest places in India. It is close to where the sacred river Ganges – regarded as the living embodiment of the goddess Ganga – springs to life. The shrine is dedicated to the river. Nearby is a rock where Shiva is said to have sat when he cushioned the impact of water falling from the heavens in his matted hair. Gangotri is accessible by bus or taxi and has several guesthouses and ashrams.

KEDARNATH: The most dramatically located of these four pilgrimage sites is also the most spiritually intense. Near the Chorabi Glacier, where the river Mandakini rises, is a rugged landscape surrounded by snow-covered mountains. The *puja* (worship) here is feverish, especially around the stone "hump", said to be left by Shiva in his guise as a bull. The spiritual potency of the place is such that pilgrims used to throw themselves from a cliff behind the temple, believing it would bring instant *moksha* (liberation). Kedarnath is reached via an 18-km (11-mile) uphill trek along a stone path from the village of Gaurikund.

BADRINATH: The last stop on the Char Dham pilgrimage is dedicated to Lord Vishnu (worshipped here as Lord Badri). The vividly painted temple, which sits at the foot of the snowy Nilkantha Mountain, is the most accessible and the most visited of the four pilgrimage sites.

Opposite, clockwise from top left:
The four abodes, Badrinath, Gangotri,
Yamunotri and Kedarnath.

MOUNT KAILASH

TIBET

THE WONDER OF IT

Resembling an enormous black diamond plugged into the earth, Mount Kailash is one of the most venerated sacred places in the world. The four sides of its mass of black rock face north, south, east and west, with a river originating from each side. Capped with a dome of ice, and rising magnificently from an immense plateau, it is, in the true sense of the word, awesome.

A MOUNTAIN PILGRIMAGE

No one has ever climbed to the summit of Mount Kailash, but every year thousands of pilgrims make the great trek to see it. It is the object of one of the most devout and flourishing pilgrimages in the world. Rather than scramble to its snowcapped top as pilgrims do on other Himalayan mountains, they walk reverently around its base. This circumambulation, known as *kora* in Tibetan, is a cross between pilgrimage and meditation and is

a practice extending back at least 2,000 years.

Circling a sacred place or thing is a ritual common to many of the world's religions. In Islam, pilgrims on the Hajj walk around the holy Kaaba seven times. The Tibetan word for pilgrimage is *neykhor*, which means to circle around a holy place. The goal is not to reach a particular destination but to transcend ignorance and materialism, reaching enlightenment by walking. Sacred sites, such as Mount Kailash, are called *neys* to remind Buddhist pilgrims of this.

Kailash is sacred in four religions: Hinduism, Buddhism, Bon (the indigenous pre-Buddhism religion of Tibet) and Jainism. Hindus believe that the mountain is the home of Shiva, the hedonistic four-armed destroyer god, and that it is where he brought the goddess Parvati to live with him. Their embrace, it is said, made the earth tremble. Buddhists consider it to be the navel of the world, its absolute centre. They also believe that it is where Milarepa, the Tibetan Buddhist yogi-sage and saint, defeated the magician Naro Bun Chung in a duel of supernatural powers that ended with a race to the summit (Milarepa won by flying to the top on a sunbeam). All four

faiths have it at the heart of their beliefs: Buddhists and Hindus circumambulate in a clockwise direction; Jains and Bonpos in a counterclockwise direction. All believe that, while a pilgrimage there is a necessary spiritual act, to set foot on its higher slopes is a sin.

Although it is easier to reach now than in the past (the drive from Lhasa takes four hours), it still takes a lot of determination to reach Mount Kailash – which, of course, is all part of the pilgrimage. The walk around the mountain takes about three days at a reasonable pace (luggage is carried by yak), although some speedy pilgrims do it in a day. Along the path are monasteries and guesthouses, hermit caves and hundreds of little cairns left by previous pilgrims.

Below: Mount Kailash, one of the world's holiest places.

THE EARTH CHAKRAS

Mount Kailash is considered to be the site of the Earth's crown chakra. The Earth has seven chakras in total, which correspond to the chakras found in the human body. The concept of chakras originates in Hinduism and is used in various meditation practices. Each chakra is associated with a certain colour. The sites of the chakras are shown here (with Sanskrit names in parentheses).

1 **ROOT (MULADHARA) CHAKRA:** Mount Shasta, California (see page 166). *Red.*

2 **SACRAL SEXUAL ORGANS (SVADHISTHANA) CHAKRA:** Lake Titicaca, Bolivia/Peru (see page 200). *Orange.*

3 **NAVEL (MANIPURA) CHAKRA:** Uluru and Kata Tjuta, Australia (see pages 86 and 92). *Yellow.*

4 **HEART (ANAHATA) CHAKRA:** Glastonbury, Somerset, England (see page 118). *Green.*

5 **THROAT (VISHUDDHA) CHAKRA:** Great pyramids, Egypt (see page 19). *Blue.*

6 **THIRD EYE (AJNA) CHAKRA:** Currently Western Europe but this chakra is mobile and will shift in the next thousand or so years. *Indigo.*

7 **CROWN (SAHASRARA) CHAKRA:** Mount Kailash, Tibet. *Violet.*

VARANASI

UTTAR PRADESH, INDIA

THE WONDER OF IT

Intense and beautiful, the holy city of Varanasi at once pulses with life and celebrates death. Its 6km (4 miles) of temples, palaces and *ghats* (stone stairs) stretch along the banks of the River Ganges, drawing millions of Hindu pilgrims annually.

LIFE & DEATH IN VARANASI

The River Ganges is India's most sacred river, and Varanasi is its most sacred city. Lord Shiva, the supreme Hindu creator/destroyer god is believed to have lived here in one of his human incarnations. Varanasi is a major *tirtha* – a Hindu crossing place between this world and the world of the gods. As such, it is a significant place of pilgrimage for Hindus, who aim to visit at least once in a lifetime to be cleansed in the river.

The city is a jumble of streets, crowded with holy men, pilgrims, tourists, sacred cows and pallbearers carrying corpses to be cremated. It heaves with humanity in all its variety and pungency. All streets lead to the river, where embankments of stone steps (*ghats*) are packed with devotees performing *puja* (prayers), *sadhus* (holy men) sitting cross-legged and children larking about. There are 88 *ghats*, most of which are used for bathing and *puja* ceremonies, while two are used exclusively for cremations.

Everything is about the river here: regarded as the living goddess Ganga, it is the focus of all rituals and ceremonies, the most significant being the acts of cremation that take place on Manikarnika *ghat* and Harishchandra *ghat*. Dead bodies are carried through the city on stretchers swaddled in brightly coloured cloths. The corpses are briefly immersed in the Ganges before cremation on stacks of firewood. The ashes are then scattered in the river.

Above: Dasaswamedh ghat, the most popular in Varanasi.
Opposite above: The sacred waters of the River Ganges.
Opposite below: Floating offerings are made to the Ganges.

MYTHS & MAGIC: SACRED GANGES

To understand why Varanasi is so sacred, you have to understand the River Ganges. According to Hindu mythology, the goddess Ganga descended from the heavens in Lord Shiva's tangled hair, then was released in streams that became the river. In Hinduism, the river is the living embodiment of Ganga: unlike other gods and goddesses, she is visible and has a physical form. Landscape and faith are intrinsically interconnected.

Rising in the high Himalayas of India at Gangotri Glacier near the Tibetan border, the Ganges flows 2,525km (1,569 miles) to the Bay of Bengal. Its holy status means that there are many temples along the river dedicated to Ganga, and Hindus believe that its waters have the power to cleanse and purify sins. The world's biggest spiritual gathering, the Kumbh Mela, takes place at the confluence of the Ganges, the Yamuna and the mythical Sarasvati rivers, once every four years. As at Varanasi, pilgrims bathe in its waters, despite it being one of the most polluted rivers on earth.

THE ORIGINS OF AYURVEDA

Ayurveda is stitched into the fabric of Indian life. An ancient healing system that emphasizes preventing illness by balancing mind, body and spirit, rather than fighting disease, it is still practised widely – often as a complement to Western medicine.

Known as the "Mother of Medicine", Ayurveda is thought to be at least 5,000 years old, although ancient Vedic texts say it is even older than that – eternal even. Its principles were said to have been handed down from Brahma, the Hindu creator god, to humanity through the intercession of other, lesser gods. Human sages and physicians then transmitted this knowledge orally to students, with therapies and practices evolving as the centuries rolled on.

The word Ayurveda comes from the Sanskrit words *ayus* meaning "life" and *veda* meaning "knowledge". Its first students studied six philosophical systems at university: logic; evolution and causality; the discipline of body and spirit (yoga); moral behaviour; pure esoteric knowledge; and theory of the atom. When the universities were closed down as India was invaded by the Turks in the Middle Ages, the practice of Ayurveda began to fade. This was compounded at the start of the 18th century with British colonization and the introduction of Western medicine and education. Fortunately, Ayurveda still had some supporters, including Gandhi, who opened the first new college for Ayurvedic medicine in 1921.

WHAT'S IT ALL ABOUT?

In simple terms, Ayurveda is the belief that body and mind are inseparable, and each influences the other. We also have a "soul", a form of energy that is linked with the energies of the cosmos. We are all separate yet linked to each other and to the universe. Our wellbeing comes from achieving balance within ourselves and within the world.

Each of us is made of five elements: aether, air, fire, water and earth. These manifest in our bodies as three life forces, or *doshas:* Vata, a combination of aether and air; Pitta, a combination of fire and water; and Kapha, a combination of water and earth. The *dosha* that dominates dictates our mind–body type. This affects our shape, weight, predisposition to illness and what food we eat. To achieve harmony we must try to balance all three *doshas.*

An Ayurvedic practitioner undergoes rigorous training that can take up to six years. They use the knowledge they gain to identify the dominant *dosha* by taking seven different pulses and closely examining hair, skin, nails, tongue, urine and stools. Specific food and herbal remedies are prescribed depending on which *dosha* is out of whack. Yoga is also recommended to balance *doshas*, as are a better breathing technique (*pranayam, or pranayama*), massage and sensory therapy, meaning the colours, tastes, scents and sounds that will have the greatest impact on an individual's wellbeing

Above: Black pepper (piper nigrum) is often used in Ayurvedic medicine.
Opposite above: Remedies are prepared in an Ayurvedic pharmacy.
Opposite below: Tea plantations beside the Muthirappuzhayar River near Munnar – a popular Ayurvedic centre.

BARABAR CAVES
BIHAR, INDIA

THE WONDER OF IT

Hewn out of granite, the walls polished to a glassy finish, the Barabar Caves are India's oldest rock temple. These four separate caves, some with double chambers, have been used as places of worship for centuries.

SACRED SIGHTS & SOUNDS

Rising from the ground like a 200m- (760ft-) long granite whale, the exterior of the Barabar Caves is itself intriguing. Draw closer and an entrance is revealed, consisting of an arch elaborately decorated with elephants, with a trellis pattern carved directly into the rock. This is obviously a place of some significance. Inside, the walls of the caves are smooth, an achievement requiring skilful masonry.

There are over 1,500 known rock-cut structures in India, but the Barabar Caves are the oldest. Dated from the Maurya Empire (322–185 BCE), they were used as a temple by members of the Ajivika sect, an ascetic faith that emerged around the same time as Buddhism and Jainism.

Apart from the stupendous feat of carving several symmetrical chambers out of solid granite, the caves present another marvel: one of them is a powerful sound chamber. Noises produced within it – chants for example – have a prolonged and ever-changing echo. Vibrations and harmonies are amplified and resonate for several seconds. Was this deliberate? The power of sound – and chanting in particular – to transcend the everyday, raise consciousness and communicate with the divine, has been harnessed by many faiths.

THE FOUR BARABAR CAVES
- Lomas Rishi
- Karan Chaupar
- Sudama
- Visvakarma

FIVE SACRED INDIAN ROCK CAVES

1 **THE AJANTA CAVES, MAHARASHTRA:** About 30 caves carved out of rock along the Waghora River. Used by Buddhist monks as prayer halls and monasteries.

2 **THE ELLORA CAVES, MAHARASHTRA:** Over 100 monasteries and temples carved out of volcanic basalt, 34 of them open to the public, in a massive complex that extends over 2km (1¼ miles).

3 **THE ELEPHANTA CAVES, ELEPHANTA ISLAND, MAHARASHTRA:** Sixth-century ancient cave temples used by Buddhists and Hindus. Still a place of worship and dedicated to Lord Shiva.

4 **VARAHA CAVE TEMPLE, TAMIL NADU:** One of the finest examples of rock-cut cave architecture, with intricate relief sculpture and carved columns.

5 **PANDAVLENI CAVES, MAHARASHTRA:** 24 caves carved between the second and third centuries CE. The main cave has a beautifully carved *stupa* within it.

KNOW A THING OR TWO ABOUT: INDIAN ROCK-CUT CAVES

In India, caves have long been regarded as sacred spaces. Many (around 1,500) have been enlarged, or entirely man-made, by carving into solid rock. These mostly had a religious purpose and were used as temples and monasteries. Some are decorated with paintings and elaborate stone carving that required great skill and craftsmanship to accomplish.

1 THE AJANTA CAVES
2 THE ELLORA CAVES
3 THE ELEPHANTA CAVES, ELEPHANTA ISLAND
4 VARAHA CAVE TEMPLE
5 PANDAVLENI CAVES

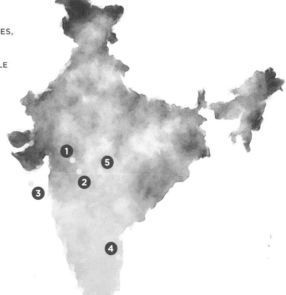

Above: A monk inside the Sudama cave.
Opposite: The entrance to the Lomas Rishi cave.

RISHIKESH

UTTARAKHAND, INDIA

THE WONDER OF IT

Hindu sages, yogis and sadhus have visited the city of Rishikesh in northern India for centuries. They have come to meditate on the banks of the Ganges and absorb its spiritual potency, practise yoga and perform rituals. Temples line the river, and ashrams draw visitors and seekers of spiritual solace and personal transformation from all over the world, including – famously – the Beatles in 1968.

TEMPLES, SHRINES & ASHRAMS

Rishikesh was put on the world map when the Beatles and their wives came to study Transcendental Meditation with the Maharishi Mahesh Yogi in 1968. Staying at his ashram, the Chaurasi Kutia, they meditated, ate vegetarian food and enjoyed a period of great creativity, writing 48 songs, most of which ended up on *The White Album*.

The "Beatles ashram" still exists, although in a dilapidated state, but it is not the only ashram in Rishikesh: the city has masses of them. An important place in Hinduism – Lord Rama came here to do penance for killing Ravana, the ten-headed demon – it is a city defined by spirituality. The Swarg ashram district is the heart of it and is where to find the ashrams, sadhus, bathing ghats and temples, the most impressive of which is the 13-storey Swarg Niwas and Shri Trayanbakshwar dedicated to Lord Shiva on the east bank. Even the suspension bridge, the Lakshman Jhula, which connects the villages of Tapovan and Jonk, is sacred: it was built at the point where Lakshmana, Lord Rama's younger brother, crossed the Ganges using a jute rope.

At sunset, temple bells ring to draw visitors to the nightly ceremony the Ganga Aarti performed on the Triveni Ghat outside the temple of the Parmarth Niketan ashram. Although increasingly popular with tourists, it is still an affecting experience as singing, chanting, music and the dispatching of little candle-bearing boats on the water are used to celebrate and venerate the holy river.

Calling itself the Yoga Capital of the World, Rishikesh boasts many yoga studios in its crowded lanes: plenty of opportunities to deepen your yoga practice and develop your asanas. The city also holds an annual week-long International Yoga Festival in March, attended by some of India's spiritual leaders.

If the crowded streets get too much, spiritual meaning can also be found by exploring Rishikesh's natural surroundings. Its situation at the foothills of the Himalayas, by a fast-flowing section of the Ganges, surrounded by forests and waterfalls, makes any ramble an uplifting experience. The more dedicated pilgrims take water from the Ganges to Neelkanth Mahadev Temple, a 7-km (4-mile), three-hour walk along a forested path from Swarg Ashram.

Opposite: Statue of Shiva on the bank of the River Ganges, Rishikesh.

KNOW A THING OR TWO ABOUT: ASHRAMS

Rishikesh and Varanasi (see page 72) have become go-to places for those seeking an ashram. There are dozens in both cities, offering people the chance to detox from the modern world: a sort of spiritual spa for those in search of meaning. The word "ashram" comes from the Sanskrit and is translated as "a step in the journey of life". In the past, ashrams were located in remote locations, where the natural setting was conducive to meditation and reflection. Instruction in religious teaching often took place there. These days, many are found in cities and offer a place to stay, vegetarian food and, most importantly, teaching in yoga and meditation. Many also insist that you undertake seva ("selfless service"): work inside the ashram or in the community. As types of yoga are numerous and varied, it's worth researching what best suits you and what the requirements of each are before turning up.

WUDANG MOUNTAINS

HUBEI PROVINCE, CHINA

THE WONDER OF IT

The natural beauty of the 72 peaks and cloud-filled valleys of the Wudang Mountains have drawn followers of Taoism for over two thousand years. Ancient stone steps lead to palaces and temples clinging to rock, where the gentle martial art of tai chi is practised and taught by Taoist monks.

A PILGRIMAGE PAST TEMPLES TO A GOLDEN SUMMIT

The ethereal landscape of the Wudang Mountains, with its jagged, mist-enveloped peaks, forested valleys, waterfalls and streams, is a prospect to restore the soul. Little wonder then that it is a place held sacred by Taoism, with its emphasis on a simple, natural and harmonious way of life.

It takes three hours to make the ascent to the highest peak, Tianzhu (or Wudang Shan), allowing time to stop along the way at Taoist temples or to simply drink in the view. Steep stone steps, worn by the feet of countless pilgrims, pass trees garlanded with scarlet ribbons and small stones, and places to buy herbal elixirs. Step away from the procession of people clambering to the top to find unmarked paths that lead to ruined moss-covered shrines and pockets of serenity.

At the summit of Tianzhu is the Golden Hall, built during the Ming Dynasty in 1416, with its carved and gilded dragons and glittering walls of polished copper. Part of a larger complex of Taoist temples and monasteries, it is associated with the god Xuanwu: a formidable deity who controls the elements and is capable of great magic.

The Wudang Mountains are also the birthplace of tai chi. A 10th- or 13th-century monk called Zhang Sanfeng, dissatisfied with the tough techniques of Shaolin boxing, sought a softer martial art to practise. Watching a battle between a huge bird and a snake, he was struck by the flowing movements used by the snake to avoid capture by the bird. Inspired, he founded *tàjíquán* ("supreme ultimate fist"), or tai chi.

Opposite: Palaces and temples cling to the side of the Wudang Mountains.

FOUR OTHER PLACES TO STOP & BREATHE

1 **LONGTOU XIANG:** Intrepid pilgrims climb out to the two twisting dragons that project over a huge drop, to light incense to bring good fortune.

2 **PURPLE CLOUD TEMPLE:** This has several halls to explore, including the Purple Sky Hall, which has statues of the fearsome god Xuanwu.

3 **NANYAN TEMPLE:** A spectacular setting, built into rock of the South Cliff of Wudang Shan and surrounded by trees, this is a good place to watch the sun rise.

4 **FIVE DRAGONS TEMPLE:** Built during the reign of Emperor Taizon of Tang dynasty (626–649 CE), it was the first temple on the mountain but is now in ruins.

KNOW A THING OR TWO ABOUT: TAI CHI

Tai chi, meaning "supreme ultimate fist", is arguably the most popular of the 300-year-old Chinese martial arts, known collectively as *wushu*. A series of graceful, meditative movements, it was originally developed for self-defence and is now practised as exercise. Like yoga, it begins with external flexibility and balance before moving inwards. As poses are repeated, your posture changes, your breathing improves, your joints become more flexible and your mind becomes centred. Energy flows upwards from the feet to the waist, chest and arms, gaining momentum on the way, until it explodes outwards through punches or kicks. Remaining relaxed through the movements allows energy to flow easily.

BATANES

CAGAYAN VALLEY, PHILIPPINES

THE WONDER OF IT

Pounded by typhoons and surrounded by tumultuous seas, the Batanes archipelago, comprising 10 islands, is an elemental place, where nature is held in awe and treated with respect. Its volcanic mountains, precipitous cliffs and rolling hills are home to the indigenous Ivatan people whose lives are intertwined with the natural world that surrounds them.

Batanes is located in the Luzon Strait near Taiwan in the northernmost province in the Philippines. The Pacific Ocean is to the east; the South China Sea to the west – the point at which they meet is turbulent and treacherous. Of the 10 islands, only three are inhabited: Batan (where the majority of people live), Sabtang and the remote Itbayat.

HOME OF THE WINDS

On the wild and remote summit of Torongan Hill on the island of Itbayat are seven boat-shaped graves pointing out to sea. In the cliffs below are caves fringed by stalagmites in which the dead were also laid to rest. This is the site of an ancient burial ground of the islands' indigenous Ivatan people. The graves look to the sea's horizon in the belief that their occupants' spirits were propelled from here to their final resting place in the ocean.

The sea and the natural world are an integral part of the lives of those who live on the Batanes. Although the majority of the population is Catholic, a healthy respect for the choppy seas that surround the 10 islands, the typhoons that rip through them, and the volcanic activity that shaped the land, engenders many nature-based beliefs. Mount Iraya, an active volcano on Batan island, for example, is the central landmark of the Batanes and regarded as "Mother Mountain". Ivatan elders say that whenever a loved one dies, a ring of clouds forms around the mountain.

Despite the high winds and geothermal activity (an earthquake in 2019 killed eight people), the Batanes islands are verdant and beautiful and can be very peaceful. Almost half of the land is made up of mountains or green rolling hills.

Limestone cliffs curl around white sand beaches and gin-clear seas. Wild horses roam the grassland of the hills of Itbayat. It is an elemental place that, despite the influence of Spanish rule in the 16th century, and the invasion by Japanese during World War II, has remained untouched by most of modern life.

The houses of Chavayan village on Sabtang Island have been built with the weather in mind. Small, squat and built of stone, they hunker slightly below the ground beneath cogon grass roofs, protected from the wind. Women still wear the *vakul* (a waist-length protective headdress), although they also weave them for tourists to wear in photographs, and men wear a traditional waistcoat called a *kanayi*.

There are no elaborate temples or grand shrines on the Batanes, just a couple of simple churches. It is the spirit of the land and its tolerant and welcoming people that sings. These islands, called the "Home of the Winds", have a spirit that calms the soul.

Opposite: Basco in the Batanes, an elemental place of volcanoes and turbulent seas.

OCEANIA

The ancestors are never far away in Oceania. They live in the mighty rock formations of Australia and in its caves and lakes. They haunt the mountains, forests and hot springs of New Zealand. They are present in both the land and in the ocean.

ULURU

NORTHERN TERRITORY, AUSTRALIA

THE WONDER OF IT

Rising from the flat desert plain, this giant mass of red sandstone at the heart of Australia is one of the world's most recognizable and potent landmarks. Sacred to Australia's Anangu people, it is compelling, otherworldly and cloaked in Aboriginal Dreamtime myths (see opposite).

Elusive meaning

Uluru is a Yankunytjatjara word. Some say it is the name of the sacred rockhole on its top; others that it refers to a Dreaming ancestor, or it may simply be a place name with no specific meaning. It refers to not just the rock, but to the surrounding land where Yankunytjatjara people live.

A MIGHTY, MYSTICAL ROCK

The mighty Uluru is astonishing in its scale and grandeur, but its size alone doesn't account for its powerful presence. It is a mystical thing, changing colour from terracotta and pale brown during the day to fiery orange-red, then purple, at sunset.

Uluru has long had deep spiritual significance for Australia's Aboriginal people. Dozens of dreaming tracks – the paths of ancestors' journeys which connect sacred places – come together at Uluru. Aborigines believe that this massive geological formation was created by these Dreamtime ancestors. It was either mud piled up by two boys playing, or the remains of a red kangaroo vomited by the Rainbow Serpent, then hardened into stone when Dreamtime ended.

Geologists reckon that Uluru was formed around 550 million years ago. Like the iceberg it resembles, the majority of it is underground. Above the surface, its bulk measures 1.6km (1 mile) in width and over 3.6km (2.2 miles) in length, and it is 348m (1,142ft) high.

The traditional owners of the Uluru-Kata Tjuta National Park are the Yankunytjatjara and Pitjantjatjara (collectively known as the Anangu) people. If you visit Uluru, respect their wishes and stay on the ground – climbing up it is now forbidden. Treating it as a bucket list destination to be conquered is counter to the spirit of the place. Instead, walk around it on the flat dirt path – about 10km (6 miles) – in keeping with Aboriginal culture. Every rock, crevice and cavity has significance: many of them have names and are sacred because Dreamtime ancestors travelled this way and performed some action there. Some caves also contain fine ancient Aboriginal wall paintings that illustrate these paths.

To discover more about the Anangu people and the natural environment, visit the cultural centre at Uluru-Kata Tjuta National Park. Made from mud bricks, it has the body of Kuniya, the python woman, built into its shape. Her body is made of mud and the roof is her spine.

Opposite: Uluru, a particularly potent place, cloaked in Dreamtime myths.

KNOW A THING OR TWO
ABOUT: DREAMTIME

Dreamtime (*Tjukurapa*) is the Aborigines' description of a time when the Earth was created by their spirit ancestors. Before the ancestors burst through the Earth's surface, it was a flat, empty place. But as they travelled across this dark world, they created its features, creatures and people through their daily activities, and gave them names in song. They also formed tribes, customs, laws and languages. The paths they walked as they did so are called dreaming tracks. Once their work was done, they returned below the Earth and fell back asleep.

Aboriginal people memorize every detail of these dreaming tracks. Most Aboriginal men can lead others across the landscape and pick out features, repeating the tales and legends in song. These "songlines" are passed down the generations and keep the spirit of the ancestors alive. *Tjukurapa* lives in the land and the people.

GARIWERD (GRAMPIONS NATIONAL PARK)

VICTORIA, AUSTRALIA

THE WONDER OF IT

Within this series of steep-sided, sandstone ridges lie caves and shelters that provide a link with the ancestral past of its indigenous people. It is a land imbued with the spirit of the creator god Bunjil and a world of sacred myth.

A DIRECT LINE TO THE ANCESTORS

Within northern Grampions National Park, near the town of Stawell, the Bunjil Shelter holds traces of the land's ancestral past. Images of hands, stick figures, symbols, animal tracks and birds painted in red-ochre clay adorn the walls like a picture book. Created by the Aboriginal Djab Wurrung and Jardwadjali people, this rock art is a direct line to their forebears.

One drawing is particularly sacred: that of Bunjil the creator god accompanied by his two dingo helpers. Gariwerd is central to the Dreaming of Bunjil. After Bunjil had created the world, including mountains, forests, rivers, plains, seas, animals and plants, he took to the air in the form of Werpil the Eagle. He swooped over Gariwerd to survey his work, then took shelter in a lookout nearby. When it came to be his time to leave the earth, he appointed the Bram-bram-bult brothers to finish his work. It was their role to name the animals, make languages and laws and bring order to the world. Bunjil became a star, keeping a protective eye on what he created.

Into Gariwerd flew Waa the Crow pursued by an angry, ferocious emu called Tchingal. Waa had pecked his enormous egg and angered him. Their tussle caused mountains to crack and release springs and rivers. Waa found sanctuary in a nearby swamp and told the Bram-bram-bult brothers of Tchingal's misdeeds. They threw spears at the ugly emu, striking him in three places. The blood that ran from his wounds turned into the Wimmera River. The emu was defeated and eaten by the brothers, enabling them to return to his egg, cook it up and create a big feast.

This is one of several creation stories at Gariwerd. The best way to learn more is go to the rock art sites with an Aboriginal guide, who will teach you about the land's cultural and spiritual significance.

Opposite: Within the caves and fissures of Gariwerd are traces of its ancestral past.

THE SIX SEASONS OF GARIWERD

The lives of the Jardwadjali and Djab Wurrung people have always been intimately linked with the cycles of nature. They divide the year into six seasons, each defined by what is going on in the natural world. The seasons vary from year to year depending on what is happening: when the wildflowers bloom, the rain may fall, animals come into season, and so on.

GWANGAL MORONN: The season of honeybees. (Autumn: late March–June.)

CHINNUP: The season of cockatoos. (Winter: late June–July.)

LARNEUK: The season of nesting birds. (Early spring: late July–late August.)

PETYAN: The season of wildflowers. (Late spring: late August–mid-November.)

BALLAMBAR: The season of butterflies. (Early summer: mid-November–late January.)

KOOYANG: The season of eels. (Late summer: late January–late March.)

FOUR ROCK ART SITES

BUNJIL SHELTER: One of the most sacred Aboriginal sites, this is the only place where the creator god Bunjil is depicted in rock art. He is shown accompanied by his two dingo helpers.

MANJA SHELTER: Stencils of small hands pattern the wall. (*Manja* means "hands of young people".)

BILLIMINA SHELTER: The ancient Jardwadjali people lived here and decorated it with stick figures and linear patterns.

GULGURN MANJA SHELTER: More children's handprints plus emu footprints.

WILPENA POUND

IKARA-FLINDERS RANGES NATIONAL PARK, AUSTRALIA

THE WONDER OF IT

This snaking mountain ridge enclosing a natural amphitheatre is of equal significance to Aboriginal people as Uluru.

A REMOTE & SACRED PLACE

There is nothing to do at Wilpena Pound but walk. A six-hour drive from Adelaide on an outback road to nowhere, it is the definition of remote. But walking is the best way to understand this spectacular landscape: hopping out of a coach and taking a snap would be to do it a disservice. Wilpena Pound needs to be discovered one footstep at a time; you need to get out on it, up it and among it.

This spectacular mountain range rises from flat farmland, a sinuous spine of jagged peaks that enfolds a natural sunken amphitheatre. Its crater-like form suggests that it was created by some mighty geological eruption or a meteor strike. It was actually formed by the layering of

sediment folded up into a mountain range: a process that began 800 million years ago. At 15km (9 miles) long and 8km (5 miles) wide, Wilpena Pound is bigger than Uluru, and more peaceful.

The Adnyamathanha people have lived at Wilpena Pound for tens of thousands of years, and it is a place of significance for them. Wilpena translates as *ikara* – "meeting place". According to Adnyamathanha Dreamtime legend (see page 87), collected in a body of stories called the Yura Muda, its steep walls are the bodies of two intertwined Akurra (giant dreaming serpents). They gorged themselves on so many people gathered for a celebration that they could not move. Instead they willed themselves to die. Their heads form two peaks: one male, one female.

There are some great treks that will take you into the heart of Wilpena Pound, as well as day hikes (a park pass is required to access the Ikara-Flinders Ranges National Park). Tracks wind their way through creeks, then climb steeply to lookouts before descending into the inner basin. It is a land rich in wildlife: you may spot eagles soaring overhead caught on thermal winds, or emus, yellow-footed wallabies

(once threatened with extinction) and euros (small kangaroos with black noses). You may also come across abandoned homesteads where early settlers attempted to farm but eventually, and after much hardship, failed. It's a reminder that this dramatic beauty can come at a cost and should always be treated with respect.

The cazneaux tree

In 1937, a photographer called Harold Cazneaux took a photograph of a solitary eucalyptus (red gum) tree in Wilpena Pound that quickly became iconic. Called "The Spirit of Endurance", this beautiful old tree (which is now protected), growing vigorously in arid, hostile conditions, came to represent the determination of those struggling to make a home in the forbidding landscape.

Opposite: The River Red Gum tree (Eucalyptus camaldulensis) known as "The Spirit of Endurance" photographed by Harold Cazneaux in Wilpena Pound.

KATA TJUTA

NORTHERN TERRITORY, AUSTRALIA

THE WONDER OF IT

Less visited and more peaceful than Uluru, although equally spiritually powerful, Kata Tjuta is a group of 36 domed, terracotta-coloured rocks. Sacred to the Anangu people, it is an important place of ritual and legend.

MYTH OF THE "MANY-HEADED" LAND

There are countless Dreamtime stories (see page 87) associated with the "Many Headed Mountain" Kata Tjuta. The highest point, Mount Olga, is said to be the home of the giant snake king Wanambi who lives in the waterhole on its summit during the rainy season, coming down when it is dry. The water channels that course through Kata Tjuta are the hairs of his beard, and the wind that rushes through the gorge is his breath. Another legend says that the domes are food piles created by the mice women during Dreamtime.

Other myths surrounding Kata Tjata cannot be revealed: this is an important site for Anangu men, who restrict access to certain areas and withhold cultural knowledge. The activities of the ancestral beings are so sensitive that not even their names can be revealed. Anangu women are allowed to gather plants and animals but only when the men are not there undertaking business. Information about Kata Tjuta and its Dreamtime legends is restricted to initiated men and is not shared with visitors.

Respect for the site and its people is, therefore, paramount. This is a place to approach gently, tread lightly, walk quietly in and keep to the paths.

Kata Tjuta, together with Uluru (see page 86) form part of the Uluru-Kata Tjuta National Park, located about 450 kilometres (280 miles), or a 4.5-hour drive, south-west of Alice Spings. The best way to enjoy Kata Tjuta is to visit at less popular times. A walk through Walpa Gorge at the end of the day (when most other visitors will have headed to the Kata Tjuta sunset viewing area) is a magical experience and is one of the shorter and easier trails around Kata Tjuta. A rocky track takes you along a creek between two of the

largest domes. Wildflowers and, if you are lucky, rock wallabies spring up alongside the path. Walpa means "windy", and a gentle breeze (the breath of Wanambi, perhaps) rushes past as sunlight floods in. Benches offer an opportunity to sit, think and wonder.

The Valley of the Winds is a longer, circular walk – 7.4km (4½ miles), or about 3–4 hours – and more of a challenge. Steeper and rockier than Walpa Gorge, it is especially lovely early in the morning as the sound of the wind and birdsong travels up the valley. It weaves its wave through Kata Tjuta's surreal domes, along creek beds and on to the Karu and Karingana lookouts.

Opposite: The many-headed domes of Kata Tjuta, an important Dreamtime site.

CAPE REINGA & SPIRITS BAY

NORTH ISLAND, NEW ZEALAND

THE WONDER OF IT

At the end of a wind-buffeted promontory on New Zealand's North Island, two oceans collide in a frenzy of roiling currents. This is, according to Māori custom, the gateway to the underworld; a *wahi tapu* (sacred place) where the spirits of the dead leap out to sea before returning to Hawaiki, the mystical Māori place of origin.

WHERE SPIRITS LEAP

On misty days at Cape Reinga, the older Māori people say they can hear peculiar, high singing "just on the edge of silence". This, they say, is the sound of spirits making their final journey from this world to the next. Sometimes they can be heard chattering and laughing, too.

This exposed and jagged rocky outcrop, perched high above the churning ocean, feels like a jumping-off point: a place at the end of the world. There is little here apart from a lighthouse and the elemental forces of nature, but for the Māori it is more than a place of raw beauty; it is also a site of great spiritual significance.

When Māori die, wherever in New Zealand they are, their spirits fly north. They are caught at Spirits Bay – in Māori, Piwhane or Kapowaitua, meaning "catch the spirit" – a verdant and sacred place of turquoise water, wild horses and mossy rocks. From there, they depart to Cape Reinga, specifically to Te Aka, an ancient, gnarled pohutukawa tree which clings perilously to the rocks. This is the spirits' place of departure – they slide down its roots and then beneath the sea to Manawatāwhi ("last breath"), the largest of the 13 uninhabited Three Kings Islands. From the island's highest point, they turn to say a final farewell before returning to Hawaiki, the underworld and land of their ancestors.

From Kaitaia, it is a 1.5-hour drive to Cape Reinga, or guided coach tours departing from Kaitaia or Paihai (Bay of Islands) will take you there and offer Māori history en route.

"I can shelter from the wind. But I cannot shelter from my longing for my daughter. I shall venture as far as Hokianga and beyond. Your task (should I die) shall be to grasp my spirit."
Tohe, chief of the Ngāti Kahu people

Opposite: The crashing waters of Cape Reinga, where the spirits of the dead leap out to the sea.

KNOW A THING OR TWO ABOUT:
THE MAORI CREATION MYTH

The Māori people arrived in New Zealand from Polynesia by *waka* (canoe) from around 1250 CE. They have no written history, but their creation mythologies have been passed down by storytellers. Although they vary in detail, the basic creation myth is the same.

In the beginning, was emptiness, *Te Kore*. Into this emptiness appeared two gods: Ranginui (Rangi), the sky father, and Papatūānuku, the earth mother, locked in an embrace. These, the first parents, conceived many male children, who lived in the cramped darkness between them. As they grew, the sons wondered what it would be like to live in the light. Tūmatauenga (or Tū), god of war, who was the fiercest, suggested they kill their parents

to find out. His brother Tāne (god of forests) disagreed and said it would be better to push them apart; then their father would remain above them and their mother would be below, nurturing them. The other brothers, Rongo (god of cultivated food), Tanagaroa (god of the sea) and Haumia-tiketike (god of wild food), joined forces to separate them but failed. Eventually Tāne managed to force them apart by pushing with his strong legs and big shoulders, and so creating *Te Ao Mārama* – the world of light. Papatūānuku wept at the separation, and her tears formed the rivers and streams. Tāne then fashioned the first humans, created the stars and brought knowledge into the world.

AORAKI

SOUTH ISLAND, NEW ZEALAND

THE WONDER OF IT

The lofty peak of Aoraki is wrapped in snow, glaciers and legend. Sacred to the Māori people, it is a place to wander and wonder.

A WORLD APART

For the Māori people, all *maunga* (mountains) are sacred, but Aoraki (or Mount Cook, to call it by its English name) on South Island is the most sacred of all. The highest mountain in New Zealand at 3,724m (12,218ft), it is permanently covered with snow, is often shrouded with cloud, has many surreal, milky lakes, and is scored with long and mighty glaciers. A formidable place of wonder and majesty.

The Ngāi Tahu tribe – the main *iwi* (tribe) of the southern region – consider Aoraki to be the link between this world and the gods: the embodiment of an ancestor who lives within it. Because of this, no one climbs to the summit of this *tapu* (sacred mountain) – to do so is to stand on the head of an ancestor,

which smacks of irreverence. (According to Māori *tikanga* – culture or lore – the head is the most sacred part of the body as it is the path to knowledge.)

In the past, burial of tribal chiefs took place in caves on Aoraki's slopes, and many Ngāi Tahu songs and poems mention it. The melt waters of its glaciers are also sacred and used in rituals around the mountain, as well as being carried to other parts of the country for ceremonial occasions. The mountain is an integral part of Ngāi Tahu life, and a constant presence.

Aoraki is one of 23 peaks of New Zealand's Southern Alps that form the Aoraki Mount Cook National Park. Easily accessible by road, it is a popular tourist destination, especially for hikers and mountaineers. There is much to wonder at here, from the towering peak itself, to Tasman Lake at its foot, and the glacier that feeds it. Because of its size and scale, it is easy to find a path to wander along and marvel at all that surrounds you.

Right: Aoraki is said to be an embodiment of a Maori ancestor who lives within it.

HELL'S GATE

ROTORUA, NEW ZEALAND

THE WONDER OF IT

An otherworldly place where the Māori underworld god, Rūaumoko, restlessly delivers temperatures that make water sputter and steam.

WHERE THE CENTRE OF THE EARTH MEETS THE SKY

The landscape of Hell's Gate is in a constant state of ferment. Its springs, geysers and mud ceaselessly steam, spurt and bubble. The smell of sulphur hangs over this otherworldly place as fumaroles (openings in the earth's crust) emit steam and gas. The ground feels fragile, volatile and thin. Some yellow pools are too hot and acidic to bathe in, and silica in rocks melts and flows like lava, scorching the earth black.

When the playwright George Bernard Shaw visited this geothermal reserve in 1934, he described it as "the very gates of hell". For the indigenous Ngāti Rangiteaorere people, who have lived here for over 700 years, however, it is a sacred place of healing. It was where Māori *toa* (warriors) came to bathe their wounds after battle and to remove the stench of war beneath hot waterfalls. Te Unauhu, a Māori *tohunga* (priest and healer), bathed daily in the hot pools with his followers in the 18th century, believing this would improve his powers of divination. It is sacred to the Māori underworld god Rūaumoko (god of earthquakes, volcanoes and seasons), whose heat boils the earth above him. And it is here, according to Māori legend, that Princess Hurutini killed herself by plunging into a boiling pool to escape her cruel husband. Her mother found her discarded robe near a boiling pool and exclaimed, *"Aue tere nei tiki"* ("Here lies my precious daughter"). The words *tere* and *tiki* were combined to give the place its Māori name, Tikitere – the sacred name that Hell's Gate is known by today.

The healing powers of Hell's Gate became widely acknowledged and, since 1871, it has been a spa. Located a 20-minute drive from the centre of Rotorua, Hell's Gate offers a range of experiences from a guided tour of the reserve to a full spa experience. Bathing in its muddy waters and hot pools is said to be good for treating inflammation, arthritis and the skin. This is not so much a luxury spa, however, more a chance to get muddy and to explore an alien landscape where cliffs steam from the Kakahi Falls (the largest hot waterfall in the Southern Hemisphere) whose waters reach 40°C (104°F) in temperature, where geysers erupt from pools to a height of over 3m (10ft) and valleys sparkle like crystal from sulphur deposited from steam.

Opposite: The sulphurous pools of Hell's Gate, an otherworldly place.

MYTHS & MAGIC: THE LEGEND OF SOUTH ISLAND & AORAKI

Aoraki and his three brothers were the sons of Ranginui, the sky father, by his first wife Poko-harua-te-po. They descended from the heavens in the great *waka* (canoe) called Te Waka o Aoraki to visit their father to persuade him to return, and to see their stepmother Papatūānuku. Realizing that they would not be separated, the brothers decided to return, but the freezing south wind was against them. The *waka* became stranded on a reef and then overturned. The brothers climbed onto the upturned boat and were turned to stone. The boat became South Island, Aoraki became the highest peak, and his brothers Ka Tiritiri, the other Southern Alps. An early name for the South Island is Te Waka o Aoraki or (Aoraki's canoe).

THE LEGEND OF NORTH ISLAND

According to Māori myth, Māui, the cleverest and most-loved son of Tangaroa, god of the sea, and Makeatutara, was responsible for creating Aotearoa (the North Island of New Zealand). His brothers, jealous of his achievements and of their parents' favouritism, decided to leave him behind when they went fishing. Māui overheard their plans and secretly made a fishhook from his grandmother's jawbone and hid himself in their canoe.

Once they had filled the canoe with fish, he revealed himself, then flung his fishhook into the sea. It sank deeper and deeper until it caught a huge fish. With the help of his brothers, he hauled the fish up. This became North Island. As he waited for his father, Tangaroa, to approve his action, the brothers, tired of waiting and hungry, cut into the fish to eat it. These formed valleys, mountains and coastline.

WAIPOUA FOREST

NORTHLAND, NEW ZEALAND

THE WONDER OF IT

A forested wonderland of giant kauri trees, sacred to the Māori people, who continue to sing songs about them and weave stories around their quiet and stately presence.

A LIVING FOREST GIANT

A short walk down a forested boardwalk fringed with ferns takes you into an ancient, green world of rare birds and towering trees. The mightiest of these is Tāne Mahuta (Lord of the Forest), a giant kauri tree (*Agathis australis*), estimated to be 1,250–2,500 years old and still growing. Its first branch is 18m (59ft) up; it has a 13.8m (45¼ft) girth and is 51.2m (168ft) tall: it is New Zealand's largest kauri. Nearby, is another giant kauri, Te Matua Ngahere (Father of the Forest), similarly stately and magnificent.

Both these living giants grow in the Waipoua Forest, a 1-hour drive from Dargaville, in a large tract of native forest which is home to about three-quarters of New Zealand's remaining kauri trees. Kauri are considered a *taonga* (treasured possession) in Māori culture and seen as the *rangatira* (chiefs) of the *ngahere* (forest). This is as much to do with practicality as spirituality: their size and strength and the timber's impermeability to sea water mean they can be fashioned into *waka* (canoes). Some of the biggest Māori war canoes (*waka tua*), which held up to 180 warriors, were made from a single kauri trunk. The trees' resin (*kāpia*) was also burned as an insecticide, wrapped in flax to make torches, used as chewing gum and mixed with animal fat and charcoal for tattooing (*tak moko*).

Many kauri have been given names and are revered, but Tāne Mahuta is the most treasured. Its sacredness is recognized by naming it after the forest god Tane Mahuta, who separated his entwined parents, Ranginui and Papatūānuku, despite their protests, by pushing them apart with his powerful legs and shoulders. Like the god, the tree's shoulders push against mother earth and its feet stretch out towards its sky father.

The number of kauri trees was depleted by logging in the 19th century. The Waipoua Forest, which was bought from the Te Roroa tribe for £2,000, is now under protection by the Department of Conservation, and no milling of trees is allowed. The few giant trees that remain, however, are threatened by dieback, a rot carried on shoes and by mammals. Visitors to Tane Mahuta must hose their shoes and make sure no soil is on their clothes before approaching it. Local Māori guides offer walking tours to see Tāne Mahuta and Te Matua Ngahere and will teach you about the native flora and fauna on the way.

Below: A Maori waka *(carved wooden canoe). Opposite: The giant kauri tree, sacred to the Māori people.*

THE HEALING POWER OF TREES

THE MOST SACRED SPECIES

For thousands of years, people of different faiths and beliefs have venerated trees. These living, breathing giants have provided shelter, medicine, heat, light and habitats for generations. They are also vital in the battle against climate change – inhaling carbon dioxide and exhaling oxygen. If any living thing is worthy of worship, a tree certainly is.

The Tree of Life, with its branches stretching towards heaven and its roots deep in the earth, is represented in Buddhism, Islam and Christianity to explain human, and spiritual, origins. The Celts believed a tree was a deity in its own right – in Irish folklore, a single hawthorn in the middle of a field is believed to be inhabited by fairies, while Druids have continued to worship in sacred groves.

The heroes of our land, some specimens have been with us for thousands of years, as silent witnesses to our activities.

KNOW A THING OR TWO ABOUT: FOREST BATHING (SHINRIN-YOKU)

Described by Dr Qing Li as "a bridge between the natural world and us", forest bathing is the simple process of walking mindfully beneath the boughs in a wood. Originating in Japan, it is a way to reconnect with nature and ourselves by engaging all the senses. By becoming aware of the sights, sounds, smells and feel of the forest, we connect with its power and begin to heal.

Opposite, clockwise from top left: Baobab tree; Banyan tree; Meditation near The Bodhi Tree; Sequoia trees.

FIVE SACRED TREES AROUND THE WORLD

1   **REDWOOD:** The mighty redwoods of the West Coast of North America are the largest trees on earth. Some are over 2,000 years old and reach heights of over 100m (328ft). They have always inspired deep reverence by California's indigenous Pomo and Miwok people, for whom felling a tree is seen as an act of violence.

2   **YEW:** The incredible longevity of the yew and its supernatural ability to regenerate have made it a symbol of rebirth and everlasting life. Considered sacred by native Britons, yews were co-opted by Christians when building churches. Many ancient specimens can still be found in churchyards.

3   **BOABAB:** The massive trunk of the baobab stores the water it needs to survive in arid conditions. In regions of Africa where everything else withers and dies, the baobab thrives. The native people of Madagascar present offerings of wine and honey to the tree, respectful of its ability to live for thousands of years. Tree spirits are believed to live within its boughs.

4   **BANYAN:** The banyan begins its life as a seed lodged in another plant. As it grows, roots descend from its branches to anchor the tree in the earth. The result is an extraordinary primordial tangle of roots and boughs. Venerated in Hinduism and seen beside many temples, the longevity of the banyan (also called *vat* or *bargad*) has made it a symbol of immortality and of the creator god, Brahma.

5   **THE BODHI TREE:** The specific tree under which Siddhartha Gautama sat for several nights, until he achieved Enlightenment, was a fig tree (*Ficus religiosa*). The state of Enlightenment is called Bodhi, after which the tree was named. The tree itself has perished over the years, but the Mahabodhi Temple in Bodh Gaya, Bihar, India, marks where it stood, and a descendant of the original tree grows at the site.

EORI, NAVADRA, KADOMO & VANUA LEVU

FIJI

THE WONDER OF IT

No one lives on these four remote islands in Fiji – lack of fresh water prevents it – but their beauty and historical importance mean they are regarded as sacred by the people of nearby island Tavua.

PARADISE ISLANDS

The only way to visit the four uninhabited Sacred Islands of Fiji is on an organized cruise or excursion. To access this *vanua tabu* ("sacred land") of aquamarine sea and white sandy beaches requires the landowner's permission. On arrival, visitors must bring a gift, or *sevu sevu*, to honour the ancestors. This is usually *yaqona* (Fiji's national drink made from the roots of the pepper plant), which is left in a sacred cave on the island of Navadra.

The four islands – Eori, Navadra, Kadomo and Vanua Levu – are sacred to Fijians because this is where their history began. Stories of the country's origins, which have been passed down orally or by dance, through the generations, tell of the arrival of Rogovaka, a big canoe carrying the first Fijians, about 2,500 years ago. A chief called Tui Na Revurevu and his people settled on Vanua Levu ("big island"), built a fortress and thrived there for a while until lack of fresh water drove them on. Archaeological excavation on the island has unearthed pottery from the Lapita culture – prehistoric ancestors of the Fijian people – that backs this up.

As the birthplace of Fijian culture, the islands are held in high regard, especially by the people of nearby island Tavua who are their guardians. It may have been a long time since humans swam in the islands' turquoise lagoons, but their land is brim full of wildlife, including migrating birds, goats and flying foxes, who have made this remote and sacred place their home.

Right: The uninhabited island of Eori, Fiji.

SEPIK RIVER BASIN

PAPUA NEW GUINEA

THE WONDER OF IT

Flowing through verdant rainforest brimming with rare plants and animal species, the Sepik River Basin is home to 430,000 people, who depend on it for their livelihoods. Traditional tribes and culture survive here, as does respect for its most powerful occupant – the crocodile.

THE SPIRIT OF THE CROCODILE

The water of the Sepik River is deep, slow and muddy. Flowing from the cloud forests of the west, it winds snake-like for 1,126km (700 miles) through lush rainforest before emptying out into the Bismarck Sea. Its vast, freshwater basin is home to hundreds of different tribes, each with its own traditions and culture. Although 95 per cent of the population are Christian, traditional animist beliefs survive. Bamboo spirit houses (*haus tambaran*) are decorated with carved figures inhabited by spirits, often in the guise of animals,

to protect them, and certain areas of the land are avoided as they are the domain of *masalai* – trickster spirits that can manifest themselves as snakes and crocodiles.

Crocodiles are central to the lives of the people of the Sepik. The river has the world's largest freshwater and saltwater populations, and they are feared but respected – crocodiles represent strength, power and manhood and feature in many legends and rituals. Each tribe has its own crocodile-related beliefs. Members of the Iatmul tribe place a crocodile at the centre of their creation myth – the Iatmul are said to have descended from the crocodile, emerging from the river as humans. When the river floods, it is said that the crocodile is shifting about; an earthquake means it is restless.

The extreme manifestation of this crocodile worship is scarification – a painful initiation ceremony, still practised in many tribes. Boys are brought to the spirit house by their uncles to have their backs, shoulders and upper torsos cut with razor blades. The skin is then beaten until it bleeds, and clay and mud rubbed in the wounds to make them protrude. The resulting raised welts resemble the hide of the crocodile. It is thought

that after enduring the pain, the young men transition to manhood and are ready for anything in life.

Travel to the Sepik River Basin is best by boat and can be organized through a local tour operator.

Opposite above: A dragon dance performed by a Sepik tribe. Traditional animist beliefs are still practised, including decorating straw and wooden houses (opposite below), with carved figures inhabited by spirits.

CROCODILE FESTIVAL

Every August, the crocodile is celebrated during a three-day festival in the town of Ambunti in East Sepik Province. Started in 2007, it has become a big draw for tourists, provides income for local people and helps to protect the environment for the crocodiles. Many different tribes from along the River gather for this cultural festival of traditional dancing and music. The aim is to keep tribal traditions alive and to display art and crafts – many with a crocodile theme – that visitors can buy.

EUROPE

Mythic tales of heroism, holiness and the supernatural permeate the sacred sites of Europe. From the inspirational life of St Francis, to the search for the Holy Grail, to the stories of the gods of Mount Olympus, each is written on the land or told in its buildings.

CALLANISH
ISLE OF LEWIS, SCOTLAND

THE WONDER OF IT

A powerful, in-between place, Callanish is a sophisticated stone circle based on the lunar cycle.

UNKNOWABLE MEGALITHIC LANDSCAPE

Scattered over a ridge on a remote Scottish island, the shimmering stones of Callanish have a magnetic pull that has drawn worshippers, archaeologists and cosmic adventurers for centuries. The stones rise, tall, pale and ghostly, dominating the barren landscape that surrounds them, casting long shadows as the sun sets. Mysterious and unknowable, they are shrouded in ancient legends and have been (and continue to be) the setting for ritual and ceremonies for centuries.

Getting there takes some determination: Lewis is the most northerly of the Outer Hebrides, and Callanish is 27km (17 miles) from the ferry at Stornaway. The journey is worth it, however – Callanish is no mere stone circle, but a sophisticated megalithic landscape inextricably linked with the surrounding hills, the sun and the lunar cycle.

It was constructed around 5,000 years ago and lay partly submerged by peat (which also helped to preserve it) until 1857. Inside the stone circle is a small, roofless, chambered tomb, built at a later date. The stones are made of the local gneiss rock, which is easily split, is in plentiful supply and contains quartz and mica, causing it to sparkle in sunlight or moonlight.

Research by archaeologists points towards Callanish having been an ancient temple used for astronomical purposes, including the recording of the lunar cycle. The regular orbiting path of the moon appears to provide reference points on the horizon, specifically along the mountain range known as Sleeping Beauty, which align with the positions of the stones.

The circle and avenue of stones create a natural setting for ritual, and several pagan customs survived until fairly recently (and are currently being reignited by a new generation of worshippers). Until the practice was banned by church ministers, local people visited on Midsummer Day, believing that "it would not do to neglect the stones" and that at sunrise The Shining One walked down the avenue, "heralded by the cuckoo's call". Celebration of Beltane (May Day) was observed in many remote Scottish places as late as the 18th century and often included walking "sunwise" (clockwise in Scotland and the northern hemisphere) three times around a stone circle. Local people came to Callanish to make their marital vows until well into the 19th century.

Opposite: Callanish was once an ancient temple. It is still shrouded in mystery.

FOUR MORE SOLAR OR LUNAR SITES

1 LOUGHCREW, COUNTY MEATH, IRELAND: An hour or so before sunrise on the autumn and spring equinoxes, a procession of people walk up a hill at Loughcrew in Ireland. They are gathering to witness the rising sun beaming along a passage in an ancient burial mound and illuminating a stone at its end carved with solar symbols. The spectacle lasts about 50 minutes as the sun passes from left to right, and is repeated over three days. This chamber tomb, known as Cairn T, is the most impressive of 32 cairns that sit on top of a range of hills known collectively as Slieve na Calliagh.

2 CARNAC, BRITTANY, FRANCE: About 3,000 standing stones that are thought to date from around 3300 BCE are ranged in dense rows, groups of several stones and *menhirs* (single standing stones) over several fields in northwestern France. The majority are organized into 11 converging rows that stretch for about 1km (⅔ mile), with the remains of a stone circle at either end. These are positioned at regular intervals, giving the site the appearance of a knobbly cemetery. None of the stones is very tall: the highest is 4m (13ft) and they reduce gradually in size along the row to about 50cm (20in). Theories abound about the stones' purpose – from a place of assembly, to ceremonial paths for funeral processions, to an astronomical observatory.

3 STONEHENGE, WILTSHIRE, ENGLAND: At the summer solstice, a motley group of druids, sun worshippers, neopagans and the merely curious gather at the stone circle of Stonehenge to watch the sun rise over a solitary large stone about 76m (250ft) away. The alignment of this, the Heel Stone, with the sun and the centre of the circle is considered proof that the people who constructed Stonehenge were sophisticated engineers and astronomers. During the winter solstice, the sun sets between three stones known as the Trilithon, making the circle of the year complete.

4 ORKNEY, SCOTLAND: In this treeless, flat, remote (and also very beautiful) place, the Stones of Stenness stand in stark relief. Considered the epicentre of Neolithic Orkney, there were originally 12 stones, arranged in a circle, but now just four stones remain. They are about 5m (16ft) high and strikingly thin, with sharply angled tops. A walk across a narrow isthmus between two lochs will take you to the Ring of Brodgar, a wide and open circle of 27 standing stones (there were 60 originally) that feels as though it's at the top of the world. Between the Stones of Stenness and the Ring of Brodgar, archaeologists are in the process of excavating a new site – the Ness of Brodgar – which includes a massive ceremonial hall and many other structures.

Above: Menhirs *in Kermario near Carnac.* Menhir *is a combination of two words from the Breton language:* maen *(stone) and* hir *(long).*
Opposite: Stonehenge continues to attract worshippers at the Summer and Winter solstices.

IONA

INNER HEBRIDES, SCOTLAND

THE WONDER OF IT

Something powerful and spiritual has drawn pilgrims to the tiny Scottish island of Iona for centuries. Ancient, holy and beautiful, it is a place that restores the soul.

A SPIRITUAL POWERHOUSE

The highest point on the island of Iona is Dùn ì, a hump in the landscape only 101m (331ft) above sea level. It may barely register as a hill, but from here there are views of some of the most ancient landscapes on earth: the island is formed of Lewisian gneiss rock, around 2,000 million years old on the west side and 1,000 million years old on the east side. Fringed with dazzling white sand and shallow coastal waters of pale emerald and cerulean blue, with carpets of wildflowers in spring, it is easy to understand why this is a holy place, a sacred isle.

Iona has long had a strong pull, its spiritual significance disproportionate to its tiny size of 2 x 6km (1¼ x 3¾ miles).

In 563 CE, Columba, an Irish priest of royal blood, was drawn here on his mission to convert heathens to Christianity. Arriving in a coracle, he established a modest monastery on the eastern shore. Columba spent his days praying, reading and writing, and his nights asleep in his cell, with a stone for a pillow. Various miracles and visions were associated with him and, by the time of his death in 597 CE, a cult had gathered around him which continued to grow after his death. In 849 CE, Columba's bones were divided and taken to Ireland and Scotland, and in 1203 a Benedictine abbey dedicated to him was built on the island – its ruins can still be seen.

In 1938, Rev George MacLeod founded an ecumenical Christian organization, the Iona Community, on the island with the aim of finding new ways to practise Christianity. The ruined medieval buildings were rebuilt and a residential centre established. The Community is still active today and draws pilgrims who come on retreat from all over the world.

The permanent population of Iona is around 120, but during the summer numbers swell as visitors pile off the ferry from the Isle of Mull – the only route to/from Iona.

Most are day-trippers who stroll through the village (no visitor cars are permitted on the island) to St Columba's shrine and to the 12th-century St Oran's Chapel, where ancient Scottish kings are buried. Walk a little farther, though, and the path will take you to quiet sandy bays with rose-coloured rocks and basking seals. Climb up Dùn ì and you will pass Tobar na h-Aois, a sacred well where, it is said, if you bathe your face three times as the sun rises, your youth will be restored. You may pass Sithean Mòr, a fairy mound, where music from an enchanted world is said to emanate. Wherever you go on Iona, magic is never far away. It is a place that recharges the soul.

The most prized pebbles on the beach at Iona are flecked with pale green serpentine and are known as St Columba's tears.

Opposite above: The turquoise sea and cluster of buildings, including the Abbey, seen from the ferry approaching Iona. Opposite below: A short walk takes you to the beautiful, unspoilt north shore.

THE WHITE HORSE OF UFFINGTON

WRITTEN ON THE LAND

The oldest of the UK's chalk horses is the most beautiful. Like an abstract sketch drawn on an Oxfordshire hillside, it has cantered over the rolling downland for around three thousand years. From ground level, it's hard to make sense of the curving lines carved into the turf, but it comes into focus when seen from above, prompting speculation that it was meant for the eyes of the gods.

The White Horse has been a place of pilgrimage for centuries. Its continued existence is testament to the fact that it has been visited and cared for by generations of people. Its outline has been kept crisp by repeated clearing of grass and vegetation, and the reapplication of chalk (a task now carried out by the National Trust). This cleaning of the horse, which dates back to 1677, occurs every seven years and is known as "scouring".

The purpose of the horse is unclear. It is 110m (360ft) long and 40m (131ft) high and might have been some sort of symbol representing a local tribe. What is certain is that it is part of an ancient landscape that runs across the Ridgeway escarpment and includes Wayland Smithy (a Neolithic chambered tomb), Dragon's Hill (a hill with an artificial flat top) and a hillfort.

The White Horse is easily accessed by car or on foot from nearby Uffington village.

Opposite: The White Horse is part of a wider sacred landscape.

1 THE WHITE HORSE, OXFORDSHIRE

2 THE CERNE ABBAS GIANT, DORSET

3 THE LONG MAN OF WILMINGTON, EAST SUSSEX

4 WESTBURY WHITE HORSE, SALISBURY PLAIN, WILTSHIRE

THREE MORE UK CHALK FIGURES

THE CERNE ABBAS GIANT, DORSET: This naked chalk man holding a club is the largest and best known in the UK – largely because of his giant erect penis. According to local folklore, a visit to the giant boosts fertility. Above his head is an earthwork known as the Trendle, where morris dancing takes place on Beltane (1 May).

THE LONG MAN OF WILMINGTON, EAST SUSSEX: A crudely drawn standing figure holding two staves (or, possibly, walking through a portal) carved into the chalk hillside. It is cleverly designed so that it appears to be in proportion when viewed from below.

WESTBURY WHITE HORSE, SALISBURY PLAIN, WILTSHIRE: Standing beneath an Iron Age hillfort, this is the oldest of several white horses to be found in Wiltshire. Records suggest that it was cut in the late 1600s, probably to commemorate an important battle.

THE HOLY GRAIL

The search for the Holy Grail has come to mean a quest for something elusive, tantalizingly out of reach. The story of the original Holy Grail is layered with myths that span back through the Middle Ages and to the life of Christ.

The Holy Grail first appears in 1190 – as a large serving dish, big and wide enough to take a salmon. It is the object of a quest in an unfinished romance, "Perceval, the Story of the Grail" by French poet Chrétien de Troyes. Other writers subsequently took up de Troyes's narrative, which involves King Arthur and his court.

Around 1200, a poet called Robert de Boron was the first to write about it (in a poem, "Joseph d'Arimathie") in relation to the Last Supper. The Grail sought, again by Perceval, was a vessel used at the Last Supper by Jesus, and then by Joseph of Arimathea to catch Jesus's blood at the Crucifixion. From then on, it became woven into many different legends involving King Arthur and his knights, who were forever searching for it, with Sir Galahad stepping up as the hero who found it in the 13th century.

One legend was that Joseph of Arimathea took the Holy Grail to Glastonbury in Somerset and buried it. It is said that the water from the Chalice Well in Glastonbury is red because it runs with Christ's blood from the buried chalice. Theories still abound about its whereabouts. Some say that it was squirrelled away to Montségur in France by the heretical Cathar sect in the 13th century. Others (including Dan Brown in *The Da Vinci Code*) suggest that it was hidden in Rosslyn Chapel in Midlothian, Scotland, or that the Knights Templar seized it from the Temple Mount in Jerusalem during the Crusades. It will for ever be shrouded in mystery, the holiest and most mysterious of all relics.

Opposite above: St Michael's Tower rises above the mist on Glastonbury Tor.
Opposite below: Was King Arthur born in Tintagel Castle, Cornwall?

WHERE TO FIND KING ARTHUR

Although the Arthurian legend lacks concrete historical information, it is still a powerful story of heroism, betrayal, magic and love. The locations where King Arthur was said to have lived and died are equally romantic, suitably mythic and worthy of a quest to find them.

TINTAGEL CASTLE, CORNWALL: Set on a dramatic headland, the remains of a castle dating back to the 5th century are said to be where Arthur was conceived and born. It has also been identified as one of the locations of Camelot (Arthur's castle and court). A sea cave below the castle is known as Merlin's Cave.

CADBURY CASTLE, SOMERSET: This hillfort is another possible location for Camelot. It has some historical credence as it was the stronghold of a warrior king called Arthur in the 6th century. King Arthur and his knights are said to be sleeping in a cave under the castle waiting to be summoned when the country is in peril, and, meanwhile, they emerge every seven years on Midsummer's Day to ride across the land at night.

WINCHESTER GREAT HALL, HAMPSHIRE: A small version of King Arthur's legendary Round Table hangs from the wall, commissioned by Edward I in 1290. The original table was said to be able to accommodate 150 knights; this one seats 24, each with his own designated spot.

GLASTONBURY, SOMERSET: Tombstones in the grounds of Glastonbury Abbey are said to be those of Arthur and his queen Guinevere. The town was once surrounded by water and is thought to have been the Isle of Avalon where Arthur was brought to be healed.

DOZMARY POOL, BODMIN MOOR, CORNWALL: This small lake in the middle of a desolate moor is said to be inhabited by the Lady of the Lake. It was she who gave Arthur the sword Excalibur, which was returned to her after Arthur's death by Sir Bedivere.

GALGBERGET LABYRINTH,

VISBY, GOTLAND, SWEDEN

THE WONDER OF IT

Were the coils of this 12-looped labyrinth intended to capture evil sprites, or as a place to gather good luck before sea voyages?

A SHORT WALK FILLED WITH MAGIC

Unlike a maze, with its bewildering choice of turnings, a labyrinth has one single path that leads clockwise into the centre and counterclockwise back out again. This one-way – unicursal – route isn't direct, though: it switches back on itself as you near its heart. Just when you think you have arrived, you are propelled back towards the labyrinth's edge. Whatever twists and turns the path takes, however, you know that it will eventually take you to the centre, and then safely return you to where you began.

The stone labyrinth at Visby on the Swedish island of Gotland is one of 40 but, with an 18m (59ft) diameter, the largest. It lies coiled on a patch of grassland surrounded by trees and open country on one side, and by encroaching urban development on the other. From a distance, it looks like a series of concentric circles raised slightly from the ground. On closer inspection, however, the circuits of the labyrinth, studded with stones, are clear to see, as is its entrance. A well-trodden path leads you into its 12 loops until you arrive at its centre. This short walk has magic in it. It transcends the everyday and gives you time to think – which might explain why the labyrinth has existed in nearly all religious traditions all over the world since records began.

Scandinavia has around 600 labyrinths, most of which, like the one at Visby, are made of stones laid on the ground. The majority of these are along the coast and, until the 20th century, were walked by fishermen before setting out to sea. Sailors followed the circuitous route to encourage good luck and a good catch: unfavourable winds were said to be snarled in the labyrinth's coils, along with evil sprites or trolls called *smagubbars*.

Gotland, which is the largest island in the Baltic Sea, has more than 40 stone labyrinths, scattered all over the island. Some date as far back as the Bronze Age, but there has been a continuous history of labyrinth building on the island, peaking during the 16th and 17th centuries and continuing to the present day. Most are of the "classical" design, a simple form that is found everywhere from prehistory onwards. As well as the many labyrinths, Gotland also has 400 Bronze Age burial mounds, 350 ship graves (silhouettes of ships outlined in stones) and 70 Iron Age forts.

The capital of Gotland, Visby, is well connected to mainland Sweden and can be easily reached by ferry or plane.

Swedish stone labyrinths are called *trojaborgs*, an allusion to the defensive walls of the ancient city of Troy, which were built in a deliberately confusing and layered way to keep enemies at a distance. (In the UK, labyrinths are frequently referred to as "Troy Town" for the same reason.)

Opposite: Evil spirits are caught in the coils of the turf labyrinth at Visby.

MYTHS & MAGIC

Legend has it that the labyrinth at Visby was created by the daughter of a wealthy but corrupt captain. He was caught and executed, but she was spared and held in a cave, with the proviso that she made a labyrinth by laying one stone down every day until it was completed. Once she had finished the task, she was pardoned.

As well as providing a spiritual maritime insurance for fishermen, the Gotland labyrinths have been used by the local community as part of midsummer celebrations. Fires are lit on a nearby hill on May Day eve to mark the arrival of spring, and games and dancing continue to take place.

ICELAND

AN EXPLOSIVE WORLD

The whole of Iceland is a sacred place; a nature temple. Raw, elemental and alive, this is a volcanic landscape of supernatural and extreme beauty. Hot gases bubble from deep within the earth, rainbow-garlanded waterfalls thunder from glaciers and waves pound ashore on black sand beaches. Volcanoes spew ribbons of red lava, and hot mud bubbles in pools. It is a turbulent land of geothermal activity, powerful, pure and precious.

Unsurprisingly, it is also a land rich in folklore. Belief in *huldufólk* (hidden people) is fairly common, with álfhól – small wooden houses – built especially for them to live in.

After Christianity, Ásatrú is the most common spiritual practice in Iceland. A faith based on the Aesir (Norse gods) and their myths, it is a reconstruction of pre-Christian Icelandic religion recreated in the 1970s. Ceremonies are held with offerings to gods including Thor, Odin, Freyr, Loki and Heimdallr. It is nature-based and recognizes the presence of the gods in all things. The mythology of the Aesir is preserved in a 13th-century Icelandic work of literature (a textbook for aspiring poets) called *Snorra Edda*.

1 REYNISFJARA BLACK SAND BEACH
2 JÖKULSÁRLÓN
3 HELGAFELL
4 GJÁIN
5 THINGVELLIR
6 GLJÚFRAFOSS

SIX THRILLING ELEMENTAL PLACES

1 **REYNISFJARA BLACK SAND BEACH:** Cliffs of hexagonal basalt columns rise like organ pipes at either end of the beach. Out at sea are Reynisdrangar, three jagged rocks created, legend has it, when three trolls were caught out too late and were frozen by the early morning sun.

2 **JÖKULSÁRLÓN:** Iceland's largest lake on the edge of Vatnajökull National Park is filled with light-blue and milky-white icebergs formed by melting glaciers.

3 **HELGAFELL:** A low-lying mountain mentioned in the Norse sagas. An ancient pilgrimage place, it was believed to be a portal to the afterlife and visited by those nearing death.

4 **GJÁIN:** A magical landscape of clear pools, waterfalls, unusual rock formations and lush vegetation.

5 **THINGVELLIR:** A 5-km (3-mile) ravine in a field of volcanic lava on the northern shore of a lake that was, until 1798, the meeting place of Althing, the world's first parliament. It is the spiritual and symbolic heart of Iceland.

6 **GLJÚFRAFOSS:** Inside a moss-covered cylindrical chamber reached through a thin crack, a waterfall plummets from a great height. As the water falls, it wears the rock into fantastical shapes.

KNOW A THING OR TWO ABOUT: THE NORTHERN LIGHTS (AURORA BOREALIS)

The spectacular night-time show that fills skies in the northern hemisphere with sheets of vivid colour has generated many myths. For ancient people, the only explanation for this wonderful but puzzling phenomenon was the supernatural. Some Sami people of Norway, Sweden, Finland and Russia still believe that the lights are the souls of the dead. The Chinese thought they were attributed to fire-breathing dragons; and in Greenland they were seen as the souls of stillborn babies. In Iceland, a sighting was said to ease the process of childbirth (although expectant mothers averted their eyes in case the child emerged cross-eyed).

We now have a less romantic but more scientific explanation. Northern Lights occur when atoms of hydrogen, oxygen and nitrogen in the earth's atmosphere are struck by solar particles, causing them to emit burning gases. (Oxygen produces green and yellow, nitrogen blue.)

THE WONDER OF IT

The turbulence beneath the earth's crust manifests itself in Iceland's primal world of eruptions, waterfalls and geysers. Rich in folklore and Norse mythology, it has a powerful and divine energy.

Above: Ethereal icebergs in Jökulsárlón glacial lake.

ANCIENT FORESTS & WATERFALLS OF BULGARIA

INTO THE FOREST

There is almost nothing left of Europe's ancient forests. Much of the magical and enriching woodland that sustained communities and incubated some of the world's most famous fairy tales has been felled and cleared. Although approximately 47 per cent of Europe is still covered in trees, it is mostly plantations of single species trees rather than the mixed forests of old.

Bulgaria was once thickly covered with dense and impenetrable woods. Travellers passing through described seeing "immeasurable and unheard of forests". The large forests of the Ludogorie region, now arable land, were called a "sea of trees" (Ludogorie's older name, Deliorman, means "the region of mad forests").

The trees that do remain, therefore, are more treasured and a reminder of what has been lost. One of these is the Granitzki Oak in the village of Granit, Stara Zagora, which is a staggering 1,600 years old, making it the oldest tree in Bulgaria and one of the oldest in Europe. Baykushev's Pine in the Pirin National Park, at 1,300 years old, is the country's oldest coniferous tree.

Bulgaria has three protected national parks: Pirin, Rila and Central Balkan, each with a network of eco trails. In the past, swathes of trees were cleared from Pirin National Park, but are now protected and so no longer threatened. As a result, a rich ecosystem has become established, and the woods are inhabited by animals including the brown bear, wolf, golden eagle and pine marten. The sanctity of the forest has been restored.

BULGARIAN WATERFALLS

Walk one of Bulgaria's waymarked scenic mountain trails, and chances are that you will come across a waterfall. The Canyon of Waterfalls in the Rhodope Mountains is made up of 46 separate waterfalls, including the highest, Orpheus, at 68m (223ft). A five-hour trek up Botev Peak will take you to the country's highest waterfall, Raiskoto Praskalo ("sprinkle from heaven"), which is 124m (407ft) in height. Easier to reach is the Boyana Waterfall on Mount Vitosha, which can be seen from the capital city, Sofia.

THE WONDER OF IT

Bulgaria's remaining ancient trees stand witness to the country's once mighty forests. Thousands of years old, they are a treasured reminder of what has been lost.

A CELEBRATED CHERRY TREE

For Bulgarians, bringing boughs of the Cornelian Cherry (*Cornus mas*), a tough, long-living tree, into the house brings good health, long life and luck. The first person (called the *polaznik*) to enter the house on Ignajden, the feast day of St Ignatius (20 December), pokes the fire with a *Cornus mas* stick for luck. On St Basil's Day (1 January) children decorate *Cornus mas* trees using *survachka* (decorated twig decorations) to celebrate the fact that it is the first tree to blossom in spring.

> "Strong nations are those that have preserved their forests, the rest have lost their roots."
> French proverb

Clockwise from top left: The eco trail leading to the White River in Stara Planina; A waterfall near Smolyan in the Rhodope mountains; Forests in Pirin National Park; Kostenski Falls in the Rila Mountains near Kostenets.

THE MEDICINAL WATERS OF HUNGARY

HEALING THERMAL WATERS

You are never far from a thermal spring in Hungary. Its many mineral-rich baths and spas offer respite, calm and the potential to ease pain. The Hungarians have long appreciated the curative and calming power of soaking in a thermal pool. Going to a spa is not seen as a luxury but as an essential element of a healthy, balanced life.

Hydrotherapy and balneotherapy are part of everyday life for Hungarians, and most cities have a thermal bath – Budapest has 24 baths and 13 spas. Four-fifths of the country sits on thermal water and it has around 1,500 thermal springs, with more than 270 types of certified mineral and thermal water, fuelling almost 100 certified health spas. Several of these were built during the 150 years of Ottoman rule and are architecturally splendid. They boast a series of indoor pools of different temperatures, from hot to a cold plunge pool in domed and colonnaded rooms lined with mosaics and gilt. Others have outdoor pools with fountains, water slides and whirlpools. There is a thermal bath for everyone, and everyone knows the importance of taking time to enjoy it.

1. SZÉCHENYI FÜRDŐ, BUDAPEST
2. GELLÉRT FÜRDŐ, BUDAPEST
3. HAJDÚSZOBOSZLÓ
4. HÉVÍZ THERMAL LAKE, KESZTHELY
5. MISKOLCTAPOLCA, MISKOLC

PREPARE TO PLUNGE: FIVE PLACES TO TAKE TO THE WATER

1. **SZÉCHENYI, BUDAPEST:** This grand bath house is a neo-Baroque masterpiece, and an elegant, and popular, place to spend a few hours bobbing about. Dip into one, or several, of its 21 pools, including a steamy outdoor one, soak in a whirlpool or book a massage or treatment.

2. **GELLÉRT FÜRDŐ, BUDAPEST:** One wing of a once-grand hotel, these baths retain the luxurious feel of Art Nouveau with glittering mosaics, fluted colonnades and indoor and outdoor pools.

3. **HAJDÚSZOBOSZLÓ:** When a thermal spring was discovered in the 1920s, the future of this city was aqua. At its centre is a spa, Hungarospa, with heated indoor baths that promise medicinal benefits, and a huge outdoor Aquapark with a water slide for fun-lovers.

4. **HÉVÍZ THERMAL LAKE, KESZTHELY:** In a volcanic crater and fed by thermal waters that bubble up from a spring 30m (100ft) below, this medicinal lake never drops below a temperature of 21°C (70°F) and can reach 33°C (91°F). Its unique mineral composition is supposedly good for arthritis and joint pain. Sufferers bring rubber rings to spend the days comfortably immersed in the healing water. Water lilies and lotus flowers on the water's surface enhance the back-to-nature feeling.

5. **MISKOLCTAPOLCA, MISKOLC:** Warm, thermal water from a mountain source flows through a 150-m (492-ft) long cave. The mineral-rich water is supposed to ease joint pain. There are also six outdoor swimming pools.

Opposite above: The warm, thermal waters of the Miskolctapolca cave bath.
Opposite below: Széchenyi thermal baths in Budapest form the largest medicinal spa in Europe.

ALL SAINTS' CHURCH, WITTENBERG

SAXONY-ANHALT, GERMANY

THE WONDER OF IT

A church door in the city of Wittenberg demonstrates the power of one man to change history. A simple act by Martin Luther triggered a split in Christianity and altered how millions of people would worship.

A HOLY REVOLUTIONARY PLACE

More than 500 years ago, on 31 October 1517, Martin Luther, a preacher at the parish church and a professor at Wittenberg University, pinned a sheet of paper to the door of All Saints' Church. On it, written in Latin, was his "Ninety-five Theses" challenging "indulgences", one of the papacy's fundamental beliefs. By paying indulgences, Roman Catholics could buy their way out of purgatory – the limbo that was said to exist between heaven and hell.

The church's original wooden portal has gone, replaced by a set of bronze doors, but the spirit of Wittenberg's most famous occupant is everywhere. The letter was translated into German and then, thanks to the invention of the printing press, quickly dispersed. A replica of it can be seen inside the church, etched into a metal panel. Luther's simple tomb can also be found here, with an inscription that begins, "Here is buried the body of the Doctor of Sacred Theology, Martin Luther".

Martin Luther (1483–1546) arrived in Wittenberg in 1508, propelled by an urge to further his religious studies (he had already been ordained as a priest) by enrolling in the monastic school. At the time, Wittenberg was a hive of intellectual debate with a renowned university that attracted the cleverest minds in late-medieval Europe, and where Luther developed his rebellious ideas. Not everyone was on his side, however. When word of his "Ninety-five Theses" got out, he was summoned to Worms by the assembly of the Holy Roman Empire to account for himself. He refused to recant, and excommunication followed. This in turn triggered the religious earthquake that was to become the Protestant Reformation.

Luther continued to live in Wittenberg for the next 30 years, preaching at the parish church (his pulpit is still there) and teaching at the university. Students gathered around his table for discussions, and it was here that he wrote further revolutionary texts. His funeral took place at All Saints' Church on 22 February 1546, and he was buried beneath its pulpit. The church is open daily and hosts religious services, baptisms and weddings. It is also a venue for sacred music events, of which Luther – a musician himself – would surely have approved.

Martin Luther was born Martin Luder. He changed his name to Luther – from the Greek word *eleutheros,* meaning "freed" – in 1517, the same year he pinned his "Ninety-five Theses" to the church door.

Opposite: All Saints' Church where Luther pinned his 95 Theses on its doors.

CAMINO DE SANTIAGO
SPAIN

THE WONDER OF IT

The pilgrimage route across Spain to the cathedral at Santiago de Compostela has been walked for centuries by Christians. Modern pilgrims tread the path for their own reasons, allowing the simple act of walking to work its magic.

A PATH TO CHANGE

This is not one single route but a network of several extending across Europe. All converge on the cathedral in Santiago de Compostela and the tomb of the apostle and martyr St James. The paths have been trodden by *peregrinos* (pilgrims) since the Middle Ages, with numbers increasing in recent years as people learn to appreciate the power of pilgrimage. At its best, the walk across Spain can be a profound, life-changing experience, and at the very least it is an adventure and a chance to step out of daily life and into something new.

The most popular route is the Camino Francés, or French Way, which starts at St Jean-Pied-de-Port and is nearly 800km (500 miles) long; it wends its way over the Pyrenees, through Navarra and La Rioja, across Castile and the plateau of Leon, over the Cordillera Cantabrica and into Galicia. The Camino Portugués, or Portuguese Way, which starts at Lisbon, Porto or Tui, is less busy, and other routes are even quieter.

Dormitories and restaurants have grown up along the path, and pilgrims carry a Pilgrims Passport, necessary to stay in designated accommodation, which is stamped at each stop. Any pilgrim walking the last 100km (62 miles) for religious reasons is entitled to a certificate called a Compostela. Many extend the pilgrimage beyond Santiago to Finisterre and Muxía, 88km (55 miles) farther, to reach the sea.

Arriving at the cathedral, with its elaborate Baroque facade, entering through Pórtico da Gloria, its main gate, is a satisfying finish to days of walking. Pilgrims pay their respects to the remains of St James behind the altar and attend mass, which is held daily at noon

Opposite above: Camino Francés – the most popular route.
Opposite below: The end of the road, Santiago de Compostela.

WHY THE SCALLOP SHELL?

The scallop shell can be seen all along the Camino, hanging from images of backpacks, used as waymarks, imprinted on churches. It is the emblem of the path, the pilgrim and St James. This could be because St James, a disciple of Christ, was originally a fisherman. It is believed that he travelled to Spain from Jerusalem to spread the word, before returning to the Holy Land, where he was beheaded by King Herod. His body was brought back to Galicia on a ship during which, one legend has it, the horse of a knight fell into the sea and emerged covered in scallop shells.

Medieval pilgrims on the Camino picked up a scallop shell when they reached the coast at Finisterre as proof that they had completed the journey. The shells were also useful as drinking vessels. The fluted shape of the shell, with all its rays converging on one point, is thought to represent the various pilgrimage routes leading to one destination: Santiago.

IN THE FOOTSTEPS OF PILGRIMS

Pilgrimage is one of the fastest-growing movements in the world. While some still walk with religious intent – to ask for a prayer to be answered, as an act of penance or as a simple act of worship – other, secular pilgrims take to the path for reasons of their own. They may have no religious faith at all, but still be seeking something. This could simply be a new, enriching experience or something more profound. Finding themselves at a crossroads in their life, perhaps, they could be seeking a new direction and a purpose.

Walking a path is a slow and deliberate undertaking and can't be hurried. It offers what modern life is short of: time. It's a chance to press pause, to give your mind a rest and to look around.

PILGRIMAGES OF THE PAST

Pilgrimages have been a common feature of most world religions for as long as they have existed. Buddhism, Janism, Islam, Judaism, Hinduism and Shintoism all place

it at the core of their religious practice. The golden age of Christian pilgrimages was the Middle Ages, peaking in the 12th century, when Christians were impelled to visit a significant site, preferably one that housed the bones of a saint or some other relic, or the tomb of a martyr. By getting close to these artefacts – and to the actual bodies – of the holy, they felt closer to God.

The three main pilgrimage destinations were Rome, Jerusalem and Santiago de Compostela. Reaching them was a risky and lengthy business. Some richer Christians even paid others to walk in their place. Pilgrimage was not for the faint-hearted: on the longer routes, illness, robbery and even murder were frequent. To keep them safe, pilgrims would carry staffs, which, as well as helping them walk, kept menacing animals (and marauders) at bay, and could be used to clear paths of foliage or other obstructions. They travelled light, taking a leather pouch or slim satchel to carry bread and documents, and wearing a broad-brimmed hat (turned up at the front to display a scallop shell), a tunic and a cloak. These items became the emblems of the pilgrim.

A pilgrimage was (and remains) a great leveller. Everyone from kings to pig farmers took to the road (as illustrated by the disparate characters chronicled in Chaucer's *Canterbury Tales*). Some pilgrimages were undertaken as penance for a sin, with pilgrims walking barefoot – some on their knees as they neared the shrine, others even in shackles.

Unlike modern times, when walking is a pleasurable choice, in the Middle Ages it was the only way to travel – apart from horseback – and the difficulty it presented was part of the point of pilgrimage. For some, a pilgrimage was the only journey they ever made, and the only time they left their own village or town.

Left: The unfurling road to Santiago de Compstela.
Opposite: a pilgrimage offers the chance to press pause and surrender to the healing power of the road.

SACRED FOREST TRAIL

FORESTE CASENTINESI, TUSCANY, ITALY

THE WONDER OF IT

There's nothing like a walk through a forest to restore the soul and lift the spirits. The trail through the Foreste Casentinesi in Tuscany takes you through ancient woodland and to sanctuaries in medieval monasteries.

A CONTEMPLATIVE STROLL

Less than an hour's drive from Florence, Foreste Casentinesi National Park is another world. Winding through its 36,000 hectares (89,000 acres) is a 90-km (56-mile) trail of ancient woodland, natural springs, moss-covered boulders, porcini mushrooms, blueberries and natural caves. Wild boar, deer, wolves, eagles and peregrine falcons live here, making their home in the wild mountainous landscape.

It has also been a place of spiritual retreat for centuries. Monks chose to build monasteries, hermitages and sanctuaries in the forests, most famously at La Verna, where St Francis received the stigmata.

The starting point of the trail begins at Lago di Ponte and it takes around seven days to walk the trail, staying in mountain huts, monasteries and small hotels along the way. The monasteries provide opportunities to pause for moments of contemplation, but the walk through this ancient, unspoiled landscape is equally as uplifting and restorative. As one monk put it: "The whole forest is a sanctuary."

SACRED HIGHLIGHTS

CAMALDOLI MONASTERY: In the heart of Foreste Casentinesi, surrounded by spruce trees, this monastery was founded by St Romualdo in 1027. Initially a hermitage in a forest clearing, it grew into a refuge for pilgrims and a monastic order, with the monastery built in the 16th century. Benedictine monks continue to live here.

CASTAGNO MIRAGLIA: This ancient, hollowed-out chestnut tree, a 20-minute walk from Camaldoli, is 300 years old and has a circumference of 12m (39ft). The tree gets its name from Countess Elena Mazzarini Miraglia who, in the late 19th century, would sit inside it to do her embroidery.

LA VERNA SANCTUARY: Perched on a limestone cliff surrounded by forest, this Franciscan monastery is where St Francis received the stigmata on 4 September 1224. A sanctuary was erected on the site and is now a place of prayer and reflection. There is also a church, a basilica and a museum.

ST FRANCIS WAY: La Verna is also where the St Francis Way (Camino di Francesco) begins. A long-distance trail – 550km (342 miles) – it links places associated with the saint's life, following a Roman road to Rome.

VALLOMBROSA ABBEY: This Benedictine Abbey was founded in 1038 and extended in the 14th and 15th centuries. Many romantic poets and writers have visited, including William Wordsworth and Mary Shelley, drawn by its mountain setting and spiritual calm. Monks look after seven arboreta through which visitors are invited to wander.

Opposite, clockwise from top left: Casentinesi forest; La Verna Sanctuary; A chestnut tree in the Casentinesi forest; Vallombrosa Abbey.

MOSQUE-CATHEDRAL OF CÓRDOBA

ANDALUCÍA, SPAIN

THE WONDER OF IT

Based on an Islamic prayer hall, the beauty of the mosque in Córdoba lies in its simplicity and repetition. There is little here apart from striped arches supported by pillars, but that is enough.

A PLACE OF PEACE AND PRAYER

Step into the mosque in the city of Córdoba and you enter a mesmerizing world of rhythmical geometry and symmetry. Unlike European cathedrals, with their soaring vaults and towering columns, the emphasis here is on the horizontal. Striped arches supported on 856 pillars recede endlessly into the distance. Intricate mosaics and painted tiles glitter and shine. It is a simple, harmonious and powerful space that feels democratic and settles the spirit – a place of peace and of prayer.

One of Islam's greatest buildings, La Mezquita (Spanish for mosque) is also part-Christian; a hybrid combination of Islamic and Western architectural styles spanning 1,000 years. Its story starts in 784 CE, when Abd al-Rahman, emir of Islamic Spain, purchased a Visigoth church built on the site of a Roman temple, to repurpose for the Muslim community. At the time, Córdoba was the capital of Islamic Spain and a cultured and sophisticated city. Abd al-Rahman wanted a mosque that represented the city's prominence in the world. What he got was a refinement of an Islamic prayer hall: a simple rectangular space divided into 11 "naves" by lines of arches in red brick and white stone. Later rulers extended the space further by adding a dome decorated with star patterns, as well as bays, arches, intricate glittering mosaics and a minaret. By the end of the 10th century, it was almost five times its original size.

The Christian intercession began when King Ferdinand II of Castile reconquered the city in 1236. He could not bring himself to level the mosque, so instead banned Muslims from the building and converted its centre into a cathedral. In 1523, King Carlos V gave permission for a huge nave and choir to be inserted into the heart of the building – a decision he came to regret. When he saw the building work in progress, he said: "You have destroyed what was unique in the world." The cathedral was only finished 250 years later: a mishmash of Gothic and Baroque styles superimposed onto the simplicity of the original mosque.

Fortunately, within its Gothic casing, the original prayer hall remains – a quiet place of calm to escape from the frenetic pace of the outside world and be still.

Opposite above: La Mezquita is a simple, harmonious space, and a place of peace and prayer.
Opposite below: The exterior of the mosque-cathedral seen across the Guadalquivit River.

MONT-SAINT-MICHEL

NORMANDY, FRANCE

THE WONDER OF IT

Surrounded by turbulent waters, Mont-Saint-Michel rises dramatically from the sea. Its Gothic cathedral sits on top of a peak of granite, its spire pointing to the heavens. Other buildings cling vertiginously to its sides. Little wonder that medieval pilgrims held it in such awe.

HEAVEN ON EARTH

There is still a pilgrimage office (the Maison du Pèlerin) in Mont-Saint-Michel. It sits at the top of the main street, the Grande Rue, that leads up to the Abbey, a reminder that once the narrow, cobbled streets thronged with medieval pilgrims, not tourists.

There has been an abbey on this tidal island off the coast of Normandy since 966 CE, when Benedictine monks settled here. For pilgrims who had walked the perilous path across the Baie de Mont-Saint-Michel, traversing salt marshes and dodging surging tides, the steep staircase to the Abbey must have felt like approaching heaven.

This pyramidal rocky outcrop, swathed in sea mist and surrounded by water, had a mystical presence long before any religious buildings were erected. Known as Mont-Tombe (Tomb Mountain), it was sacred to the Celts, who believed it was a portal to the afterlife. Its current name was coined in 708 CE, when Aubert, the Bishop of Avranches, had a vision. Archangel Michael instructed him to build an oratory on the rock – which, despite initial reluctance, he did, in 709 CE. St Michael has remained a spiritual presence ever since: a gold statue of him slaying the dragon stands on top of the abbey's spire. Pilgrims prayed to him for protection against the devil and to assist them at the hour of their death.

Two decades later, the Benedictines battled against the sheer granite rock, gravity and the elements, to build their monastery. Their determination won through and, despite the initial church collapsing, an abbey was built. In 1228, monks' living quarters known as the Merveille ("The Marvel") were built and clung vertiginously to the rock face, supporting the structure above. The Abbey became a centre of learning, attracting writers and manuscript illustrators. A village grew up alongside and other, smaller chapels were built.

Pilgrimage to Mont-Saint-Michel faltered during the Reformation, and very few monks remained by the time of the French Revolution. In 1791 the Abbey was closed and became a prison, until that was closed by Napoleon III in 1863 and the building renovated. Christian worship began again in 1922.

To reach Mont-Saint-Michel, you could leave your car at the car park on the mainland 2.5km (1½ miles) from the island, and catch a shuttle bus. It's much better to walk, though. It can be reached easily except for six or seven times a year for a few hours at exceptionally high tides. A tree-lined footpath from the car park along the Couesnon River and a wooden boardwalk will take you there. Approach it steadily and gently and the majesty of the place will slowly be revealed.

Opposite: The approach to Mont-Saint-Michel with the spire of its Abbey pointing towards the heavens.

SANCTUARY OF OUR LADY OF LOURDES

LOURDES, FRANCE

THE WONDER OF IT

Millions of pilgrims travel to Lourdes every year, drawn by the miraculous visions of a young girl. The city has become a manifestation of Catholic faith fuelled by the power of prayer.

A CITY BUILT ON FAITH

In 1858, the small town of Lourdes in the Hautes-Pyrénées region of southwestern France found itself at the centre of religious fervour. On 11 February, a 14-year-old girl, Bernadette Soubirous, was collecting firewood by the river when a white-robed woman appeared to her in a grotto. The woman revealed herself to be the Virgin Mary with the words "*Que soy era Immaculada Councepciou*" ("I am the Immaculate Conception"). She reappeared 18 times, directing Bernadette to scratch at the earth with a stick and drink from the spring that bubbled up. When word got out, people came to be healed at the spring, and many miracles were said to have occurred.

Despite the Church's initial caution and request for evidence, news of the miracles spread, and Lourdes became a place of mass pilgrimage. Now, more pilgrims come here than to any other place in the world, including Rome and Mecca. A great religious city has grown up where Bernadette saw her visions. Not everyone comes to be healed – some come simply to pray to the Virgin Mary, as an act of penitence or in gratitude for a prayer fulfilled.

The Sanctuary of Lourdes (or Domain as it is commonly known) comprises several churches, including the underground Basilica of Saint Pius X, which can accommodate 20,000 people: more than the population of the city.

The focus for most pilgrims, however, is the Grotto of Massabielle, or Cave of Apparitions, where Bernadette had her visions. The actual spot of the visions is marked by a statue of the Madonna carved in marble, and the original spring can be seen at the back of the grotto. An underground waterway channels the water to fountains and pools downstream, where pilgrims immerse themselves, hoping to be healed. Thousands have claimed that a miracle has occurred for them, although only 69 have been confirmed by Lourdes's Bureau of Medical Observations.

Every night at 9pm, a torchlight procession winds its way through the city to the grotto as pilgrims sing the *Ave Maria*. It is a profoundly peaceful and moving expression of faith and of hope.

In 1866, Bernadette's visions were declared real by The Vatican. She left Lourdes that year to go to Nevers, near Paris, and become a nun. She died in 1879, aged 35, and was made a saint in 1933.

Opposite: The Basilica of the Immaculate Conception where Bernadette saw her visions of the Virgin Mary.

ES VEDRÀ

IBIZA

THE WONDER OF IT

About 2km (1¼ miles) off the coast of Ibiza lies the mysterious, uninhabited island of Es Vedrà. Wreathed in myths, it is said to be the birthplace of a goddess, the home of sirens and sea nymphs and the centre of a magnetic force.

A MYTHIC ISLE

At sunset, people gather on the cliffs above the beach of Cala d'Hort on the southwest coast of Ibiza and look out to sea. This is when the small, uninhabited island of Es Vedrà looks its most bewitching. As the sun drops behind its distinctive cleft profile and the sea shimmers with gold, it feels as though there is magic in the air.

Es Vedrà has the power to evoke thoughts of wonder and mystery, its mystic presence generating countless myths and legends. Its rocky peak has been described as the tip of the lost civilization of Atlantis. The sirens and sea nymphs who tried to lure Odysseus from his ship in Homer's *Odyssey* were

said to hang out on Es Vedrà. Some say it is the third most magnetic spot on earth, after the North Pole and the Bermuda Triangle, and that navigational instruments are affected by it, although there is no scientific evidence to back this up. Others claim they have seen UFOs and flashing lights hovering above it. A popular local *rondalle* (fable) concerns two brothers who went to the island to collect samphire to cure their father's illness and found they had to contend with a giant who was living in one of the many caves.

A Carmelite friar, Francisco Palau y Quer, lived on the island for a short while in 1855, and had visions of a beautiful woman dressed in white. Identification of this vision of loveliness is sketchy, but it could have been the goddess Tanit – Es Vedrà is believed to be the birthplace of Tanit, who remains a powerful presence on the island. Around 600 terracotta images of her were found in a modest little cave, Cova d'es Cuieram, on a remote corner of Ibiza itself. Dating from the 5th to the 2nd century CE, they are evidence of the importance placed on worship of the goddess by the island's ancient people. Reverence for her continues – votive offerings are still left in the cave.

It is not possible to land on Es Vedrà, but you can get close to it on a boat trip leaving from the resort of San Antonio on Ibiza.

"When the end of the world comes, I should like to be on Ibiza."
Nostradamus

Opposite: Es Vedrà – bewitching and mysterious.

GODDESS GUIDE: TANIT

Many women are drawn to Ibiza's feminine energy, which is particularly present in the Cova d'es Cuieram, where the goddess Tanit is worshipped. Tanit was a Phoenician goddess of sexuality, fertility and death, also known as Astarte, who was associated with ritual acts of fertility, including orgies. She was worshipped in Ibiza until the Roman emperor Vespasian suppressed her cult in 74 CE. Despite this, veneration of her continued and there are still statues of her on the island.

PAMUKKALE

DENIZLI, TURKEY

THE WONDER OF IT

The thermal waters of Pamukkale cascade down a ghostly hill into limpid aquamarine pools. Above them is Hierapolis, a ruined Roman spa, once also a place of healing.

ETHEREAL THERMAL TERRACES

A footpath leads the visitor up past travertine terraces and aquamarine pools of warm, clear water. Stalactites formed by centuries of calcium-rich thermal water dripping slowly down the mountainside hang in sculptural forms. This is an ethereal place where magic is sure to happen.

Pamukkale has drawn the sick and the weary to its hot thermal springs since classical antiquity. Its terraces have built up over millions of years from the gradual deposition of limestone by thermal springs as they spurt and then pour over the mountain.

Not surprisingly, they continue to draw crowds. These days, visitors are restricted to the footpath and must be barefoot: too many feet have polluted and eroded the terraces and pools in the past. The quietest time to visit is in the morning: it's worth staying locally in the village to get there bright and early, as most day-trippers drive from the coast and arrive in the afternoon. Bring a swimsuit – splashing in the pools is off limits but another thermal experience awaits: a dip in the Antique Pool of Hierapolis.

Hierapolis ("Holy City" in ancient Greek) was a Roman city, founded in 190 BCE, and built around the thermal waters. The hot springs – with temperatures ranging from 35°C (95°F) to 100°C (212°F) – were thought to have curative properties, and people came to bathe in their mineral-rich waters. At its height, the city must have been spectacular. Even now, in ruins, it is impressive. Built on a grid, the Hierapolis was designed with the needs of its citizens in mind. The impressively grand amphitheatre could seat more than 12,000 spectators, and a necropolis outside the city's boundaries has 1,200 tombs and sarcophagi.

At the Temple of Apollo, eunuch priests tended to the oracle, whose power was said to come from a foul-smelling spring in a nearby cave. Called the Plutonium (after Pluto, god of the underworld), it emitted poisonous vapours, including carbon dioxide, a result of subterranean geological activity.

One of the pleasures of visiting is that you can bathe in the Sacred Pool (also called the Ancient Pool), filled with mineral-rich water as warm as 36°C (97°F) as the Romans once did. You also get to swim among

submerged columns – which toppled into the water during an earthquake.

Most visitors are day-trippers from nearby Mediterranean resorts, but the best way to visit is by car (about a 3-hour drive from Kusadasi) and stay overnight in Pamukkale village, then explore the ruins the following morning before the crowds start to descend.

Above: Hierapolis was built around thermal waters by the Romans who considered it a holy place.

MOUNT IDA (PSILORITIS)

CRETE

THE WONDER OF IT

It's hard to miss Mount Ida, as it rises from the centre of Crete, dominating the landscape. But it's not its size that makes it sacred: this is the birthplace of the god Zeus.

GOD-LIKE MOUNTAIN

At the heart of Crete is the holy mountain range of Psiloritis, with Mount Ida its highest peak, from which the entire island can be seen spreading out. Dominating the landscape, Ida is never out of sight. Hikers make their way through the remains of pine forests, along gorges and through ravines to its barren, sometimes snowcapped, summit. On 14 September every year, Christian pilgrims climb a rocky path to a small stone chapel, the Church of the Holy Cross, to sleep on the summit (Timios Stavros) and celebrate the day of the Holy Cross at mass the following morning.

CRETAN MYTHOLOGY: A MONSTROUS BULL, A LABYRINTH & A THOUGHTLESS BETRAYAL

In Greek mythology, Crete was the island of King Minos, a tyrant who kept the Minotaur – a beast with a bull's head on a man's body – hidden within a labyrinth. The monstrous animal was fed on a diet of seven Athenian youths and maidens per year. They were sacrificed in payment for the slaying of Minos' son by the Athenians. On the third year, Theseus, son of King Aegeus, volunteered to go instead of the group of hostages. Minos' daughter Ariadne fell in love with him and gave him a ball of wool to guide him out of the labyrinth. Theseus fled with Ariadne, but then deserted her on the island of Naxos. As he sailed into Athens, he forgot to hoist a white sail on his ship – which he had promised his father to do as a sign that he was still alive – and Aegeus killed himself by throwing himself into the sea.

All of this would be enough to render the mountain sacred, but there is another, even holier, reason. On its eastern slopes is the Idaean Cave which, according to myth, is the birthplace of Zeus (see right). Held sacred by the Minoan people, it was a place of veneration, ritual and initiation. Votive offerings are still left inside the chambers of the limestone cavern.

The sacred Idaean Cave (opposite) is on the eastern side of Mount Ida, above.

RHEA GODDESS GUIDE

How Zeus came to be raised in a cave on the side of Mount Ida is the stuff of Cretan mythology. His mother, Rhea, was the daughter of the earth goddess, Gaia, and the sky god, Uranus, who had 12 children, known as the Titans. One of Rhea's brothers was Cronus, whom she married.

A prophet told Cronus that one of his children would betray him, so, when the first five were born, he swallowed each of them at birth. Pregnant with her sixth child, Rhea was determined to save him. At the baby Zeus' birth, she presented her husband with a rock wrapped in a blanket instead of a baby. Cronus was fooled and he swallowed it.

Rhea took Zeus to Crete and hid him in a cave, where he was raised by the goat nymph Almatheia and guarded by the Kouretes, a bunch of warriors who drowned the baby's cries and kept him safe from Cronus with their noisy war dances. As foretold, Zeus grew up and returned to defeat his father in battle.

(For the next instalment, see What Happened Next, page 148.)

MOUNT OLYMPUS

MACEDONIA, GREECE

THE WONDER OF IT

This imposing ridge of jagged mountains feels like the top of the world. No wonder the ancient Greeks believed it was where the gods lived: it links this realm and the divine.

THE HOME OF THE GODS

To the ancient Greeks, the loftiest peaks in the country, with their snowcapped, barren summits far above the clouds, were the land of the gods. The many-ridged Mount Olympus, and the highest peak of all, Mytikas, were where the 12 Olympian gods (Zeus, Hera, Poseidon, Demeter, Athena, Apollo, Artemis, Ares, Aphrodite, Hephaestus, Hermes and Hades) surveyed the world beneath them. Zeus held court from his throne on the peak known as Stefani, advising heroes from Greek mythology who clambered up to seek his counsel, looking down upon the feeble activities of mere mortals, and delivering thunderbolts and lightning when displeased.

Every so often, the gods came down from the mountain and participated in earthly affairs. Lusty Zeus disguised himself in various forms to seduce mortal women: he approached Leda as a swan, Europa as a bull and Danaë in a shower of gold. Apollo fell in love with the forest nymph Daphne (at The Spring of Daphne, at the foot of the mountain), which ended badly as she was turned into a laurel tree. And Demeter lived among humans disguised as an old woman when she was mourning her daughter Persephone.

A climb to the highest peaks of Mount Olympus, with its plunging gorges and teetering rocky outcrops, may be out of reach for some of us, but a walk in its verdant foothills is a rewarding – even divine – experience.

> **The Chapel of the Prophet Elias**
> Built on a peak near Mytikas, this chapel was founded in the 16th century by Saint Dionysus, an ascetic monk, who was said to have lived in it from time to time.

Above right: Hera, one of the 12 Olympian gods who lived on Mount Olympus, opposite.

WHAT HAPPENED NEXT

When Zeus became a man, he freed his five siblings, whom Cronus, his father, had swallowed, by making Cronus vomit them up. An epic battle between the old guard (the Titans led by Cronus) and the new (the Olympians led by Zeus) began. There was much at stake: the winners would rule the universe. After 10 years of fierce fighting, the Olympians claimed victory. From their base on Mount Olympus, Zeus and his siblings divided up Creation. Poseidon got the sea; Hades the Underworld; and Zeus the sky and the weather. Zeus was also the chief deity of the Olympians.

THE ACROPOLIS

ATHENS, GREECE

THE WONDER OF IT

This city of temples overlooking Athens is a three-dimensional monumental devotion to the warrior goddess, Athena.

THE ANCIENT CAPITAL OF THE WORLD

High above the city of Athens, on a limestone hill, stands the Acropolis, a city of temples devoted to one goddess: Athena. Athena was worshipped throughout Ancient Greece, and nowhere more so than in the city that bore her name.

The Acropolis was built in the 5th century BCE during the Golden Age of Athens, when the city was at its cultural peak. Pericles, its general, spared no expense in honouring the goddess. The country's best architects and sculptors were employed in a project that took 50 years to complete and that still looks spectacular today, despite its ruined state.

The crowning glory of the Acropolis is, of course, the Parthenon. This mighty Doric temple devoted to Athena can be seen from all over the city and has become an emblem

of Greece. The skeleton of the structure, which still stands, is eight Doric columns at each end and 17 on either side. Above the columns, decorative panels showed scenes from battle: the Olympian gods fighting the giants; the battle between the Ancient Greeks and the Amazons; the fight between the Lapiths and the Centaurs; and the sacking of Troy. Many of these panels were destroyed during an explosion in 1687, or were removed. The best-preserved are in the British Museum, London.

At the heart of the Parthenon, in an inner chamber, was the most splendid item of all: the statue of Athena. Made of gold and ivory with a wooden core and jewelled eyes, it was almost 12m (39ft) high. Resting on her right hand was the winged goddess of victory, Nike, and in her left hand, a spear. At her feet were a shield and a serpent. The work of Phidias, Ancient Greece's foremost sculptor, it was considered one of the wonders of the world. A fitting tribute to the goddess who defined the city and the nation, it vanished when it was removed and taken to Constantinople (where it was mentioned in a 10th-century account).

THE BIRTH OF VENUS

Like many characters in Greek mythology, Athena had an unusual start in life. Metis, Zeus's first wife, became pregnant. Zeus had been told that any children of Metis would be wiser than their father. Terrified that the child might overthrow him (as he had done with his own father, Cronus), Zeus swallowed Metis whole. Some time later – after he had married six other women – he started to have terrible headaches. Unable to bear the pain, he asked Hephaestus to cleave his head open with an axe, whereupon Athena jumped out, fully grown and wearing armour. Zeus was delighted and Athena became his favourite child.

ATHENA GODDESS GUIDE

A fierce warrior who advised many Greek heroes in the strategy of war, Athena is a most suitable goddess to protect Athens. Stern, beautiful and ready for battle, she is usually represented wearing armour and a helmet and carrying a shield and a spear. An owl often sits beside her – a symbol of her wisdom. Unlike most of the amorous Greek pantheon, Athena is a virgin. She is also the goddess of weaving, pottery and sculpture.

Every year in Ancient Greece, the Panathenaia, a festival celebrating Athens and its goddess, was held. Every fourth year, a Panathenaic Procession took place where a new *peplos* (shawl) was made to clothe the statue of Athena. This was carried through the streets on a cart. The procession can be seen carved in stone on the Parthenon frieze, now in London's British Museum.

Left: The Erechthenion – one of the temples on the Acropolis dedicated to Athena and Poseidon.

THE SEARCH FOR ATLANTIS

The legend of Atlantis – a utopian city lost beneath the sea – is a potent one. Packed with myths, wonder and mystery, it has intrigued writers, scientists and explorers for centuries.

Its story begins with an account written by the Athenian philosopher Plato in 330 BCE. According to him, this city with its majestic palace, hot and cold running water, elephants, bulls and 10,000 chariots, was located at the Pillars of Hercules – the two rocky promontories that marked the entrance to the Strait of Gibraltar and the Mediterranean. Atlantis was a powerful naval state, but even so, wrote Plato, it was defeated in battle by his Athenian forebears, after which it sank into the sea and was never found again.

This account prompted numerous theories about the existence of Atlantis and its possible location that were taken up by Renaissance writers, and that have continued into modern times.

In 1882, American writer and amateur scientist Ignatius L Donnelly published *Atlantis: The Antediluvian World*, which claimed that Atlantis was a lost antediluvian (pre-biblical Flood) continent which had contributed to the emergence of Mayan and Egyptian cultures. This prompted interest from various pundits who attributed other wonders to Atlantis, including aircraft, submarines and assorted sophisticated technologies.

In 1940, the American clairvoyant Edgar Cayce predicted that the lost continent of Atlantis would start to rise again in 1968 or 1969 off the east coast of North America. He claimed that Atlantis had been the first civilization and that Atlanteans used crystals and sound waves for healing, and were skilled at telepathy, psychokinesis and astral projection. He believed that the downfall of Atlantis was the result of its people's greed and in-fighting, but that before it disappeared into the sea, many of them fled to Egypt.

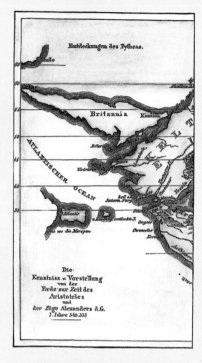

Atlantis as mapped by Ignacy Lelewel, 1831.

In 1968, some aircraft pilots reported glimpses of what looked like walls or building foundations 80km (50 miles) off the Florida coast among a tiny archipelago of islands. A worldwide stir followed: could this be the Atlantis that Edgar Cayce had predicted would rise again? Divers explored 11m (36ft) down and found huge, square, white blocks that looked as though they were a man-made road on the seabed. Further inspection by scientists, however, revealed that they were an entirely natural formation and had never been part of a landmass.

Nevertheless, the search for Atlantis continues. One theory has it that a massive volcanic eruption on the Greek island of Santorini led to an enormous tsunami that could have caused the sinking of Atlantis. Other speculation has placed it in the sea near Sardinia, Malta, Crete, Cyprus, Indonesia, Morocco, even Antarctica. If it is beneath the ocean in any of these places, it is keeping itself well hidden.

"There were violent earthquakes and floods, and in a single day and night of misfortune...the island of Atlantis slipped into the sea."
Plato, Timaeus and Critias

Opposite above: The island of Santorini, Greece – could this be the location of Atlantis? Opposite below: Atlantis is thought to exist in the waters beneath the volcanic islands in Greece.

NORTH AMERICA

The ancestors are never far away in the mountains, lakes and valleys of North America, it's just a question of looking for them. Their presence can be felt in the ancient dwellings of the Pueblo peoples, the fathomless depths of Crater Lake, the sacred volcanoes of Hawaii and the vast wilderness of the Arctic.

MESA VERDE, MONTEZUMA COUNTY

COLORADO, UNITED STATES

THE WONDER OF IT

On a high plateau in Colorado are the ruins of its Ancestral Pueblo people. A place of architectural wonder, it is also a site of spiritual veneration.

IN THE HOUSES OF THE SPIRITS

No one knows why the Ancestral Puebloans left the pueblos of Mesa Verde in the 13th century. Speculation suggests it was because of a severe drought, or possibly a violent attack. What is known is that they left behind buildings of great structural complexity and skilful construction. These clusters of dwellings lay forgotten for hundreds of years, until a Quaker rancher called Richard Wetherill stumbled upon them in 1888, when he was out looking for stray cattle. A local Ute tribal leader, Chief Acowitz, warned him to stay away: "When you disturb the spirits of the dead, you die too," he said. Wetherill ignored

his warning, and his discovery led to the establishment of a national park. Now visitors can clamber around these clusters of rooms hewn into the sandstone cliff face and get a sense of what life was like for their ancient occupants living in this land of plunging canyons and snowy peaks.

The Ancestral Pueblo people (previously known as Anasazi Puebloans – see page 158) lived at Mesa Verde for around 700 years, from 600 to 1300 CE. As they became more established, their buildings became more ambitious. The earliest dwellings were simple pit houses dug a metre (a few feet) or so into the earth. Later on, multiple-chambered structures such as Cliff Palace and Spruce Tree House were carved into the rock and included many *kivas* – sunken communal rooms used as places of worship.

The Ancestral Puebloans were a peace-loving people with a deep respect and connection to the landscape around them. They gathered around fires in *kivas* to commune with the great spirits and with the *kachina* (see opposite). A small hole in the floor called a *sipapu* symbolized the portal through which

their ancestors emerged to enter the world and was used as a means to communicate with them. The number of *kivas* per person at Mesa Verde indicates how central the world of the spirit was to daily life.

There are nearly 5,000 archaeological sites at Mesa Verde, including 600 cliff dwellings. Most visitors head to Cliff Palace, the largest cliff dwelling in America, or Balcony House, and scramble through surprisingly small entrances – the height of the average Ancestral Puebloan man was 1.7m (5ft 6in); women were around 1.4m (5ft) – and up ladders to get a glimpse of what life was like on this high plateau in America's southwest.

Visitors can expect to pay a park entrance fee, and some cliff dwellings require tickets which must be purchased in person.

Below: Cliff Palace, the largest cliff dwelling in Mesa Verde National Park.

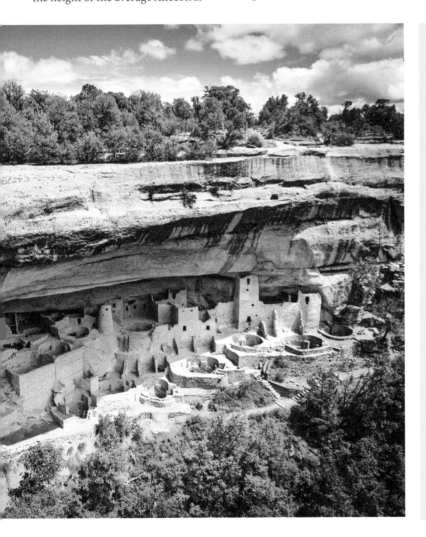

KNOW A THING OR TWO ABOUT: KACHINA

The central belief of the Ancestral Pueblo people, particularly the Hopi, is that everything has a spirit. *Kachina* are the personification of these spirits and can represent anything in the natural world or cosmos, from an ancestor or a location to a natural phenomenon. There are *kachina* for the sun, stars, thunderstorms and insects. They are not worshipped, but are considered powerful and benevolent beings who can help with everyday tasks. In addition, they can be represented as small dolls, and are also impersonated by men who dress up in costumes and masks to perform ceremonial dances.

CANYONS OF THE ANCIENTS

COLORADO, UNITED STATES

THE WONDER OF IT

Barely touched for over 1,000 years, the remnants of the ancestral Pueblo civilization that lie scattered over the land provide a direct link to their lives and their spirit.

ANCESTRAL HOMELAND

The high desert of Colorado, before you reach the Rocky Mountains, is a raw, rugged and remote place. At first it appears as though there is nothing much there apart from the distinctive *mesas* (flat-topped hills), scrubby bush, rough roads and shallow canyons. But on further investigation, another world is revealed: that of the ancestral people who lived here more than 1,000 years ago.

All over the 71,247 hectares (176,056 acres) of the Canyons of the Ancients National Monument are the remnants of the culture of the Anasazi Puebloans. Their culture flourished in the Four Corners area (where four states – Colorado, Utah, Arizona, New Mexico – meet) between 300 CE and 1300 CE, and its traces are everywhere. Over 6,000 archaeological sites have been recorded – most untouched since that time. Only three sites have been restored; the rest have been left undisturbed (locations of the undeveloped sites are not publicised to prevent large visitor numbers). The park is massive and relatively unvisited, so it's easy to find a deserted spot and to experience what it must have been like to live here, and to feel a connection with the past and its people.

It's also a chance to marvel at the skill of the ancestral stone masons as you explore the villages with towers, shrines and *kivas* (underground chambers built for spiritual ceremonies).

The three restored sites are a good place to start: Lowry Pueblo was constructed around 1060 CE and is reached via a 14km- (9 mile-) long road. Many people lived here: there are 40 rooms, some built as high as three floors, as well as eight *kivas* and a Great Kiva, which was built later, in 1103 CE. This is an impressive building – large, circular and subterranean – and was where people from all around gathered for religious ceremonies and celebrations. Sand Canyon Pueblo was the largest settlement in the area and was built later, in the 13th century. There are many family blocks here – it is estimated that 750 people lived in the pueblo, grouped in clusters – as well as 100 *kivas* (most families had their own) and 14 towers. All structures are impeccably built from carefully chiselled stone blocks. The third site, Painted Hand Pueblo, has the best surviving circular tower, which was built on top of a projecting rock. It is also notable for its faint handprint pictographs.

Although this is an abandoned landscape, it is also a living one. The homeland of many Pueblo peoples, who return to communicate directly with their ancestors, it is a wild and sacred place occupied now by the spirits of the past.

Opposite: The circular tower of Painted Hand Pueblo.

KNOW A THING OR TWO ABOUT: SWEAT LODGES

As well as *kivas*, there is evidence of other sacred structures built at the Canyons of the Ancients: sweat lodges. Usually constructed from natural materials, most of these have long since vanished, but traces remain. Modern interest in indigenous culture and spiritual practices has generated an increase in non-Native American people participating in sweat lodges, but what does it involve?

Most sweat lodges are built from flexible pieces of wood hooped over to form a dome, then covered with a breathable fabric, like blankets. A fire is built outside the entrance and rocks are heaped upon it. A small number of participants (10–12 is about right) are cleansed first in a smudging ceremony (see page 161). Then they gather inside as the first hot rocks are brought in. Light is extinguished. A Native American elder leads the proceedings as, one by one, everyone speaks of their reason to be there. The elder then tells stories, sings or drums as the heat increases. Progressively hotter rocks are introduced in stages, usually with 15-minute breaks inbetween. Water is poured onto the rocks to create steam. At the end of the sweat, participants plunge into cold water, preferably a nearby stream.

A sweat lodge should be conducted with reverence for Native American tradition. There are real dangers if it is not handled well, not just psychically but physically – the unaccustomed heat can cause dehydration and, if the lodge is not well ventilated, suffocation. But if it is practised as it should be, it is also a powerful tool for prayer, purification and healing.

SEDONA

ARIZONA, UNITED STATES

THE WONDER OF IT

Within the beautiful red sandstone mountains and *mesas* surrounding Sedona are "vortexes" – said to be repositories of uplifting energy – that have drawn spiritual seekers for centuries.

SPIRITUALLY UPLIFTING ENERGY

The whole of Sedona is a magical kingdom. Surrounded by towering blood-red rocks rising in jagged formations, it feels like a setting for a mythical adventure – even more so at sunrise when the red sandstone is illuminated by the sun and glows brilliant orange against the blue, blue sky. Little wonder then that it has become the New Age capital of the United States, a magnet for spiritual seekers of all varieties drawn by the spectacular landscape and the "vortex sites" within it.

Sedona's spiritual lure isn't new, however: it spans centuries. The ruins of the Sinagua people, who lived here from around 650 CE,

circle the city. It is thought that they lived on the outskirts and travelled into the land of red rocks for sacred ceremonies. They left rock art, pueblos and cliff dwellings before abandoning the valley in 1400. Other native tribes came as well: the Yavapai from the west, around 1300; and the Apache, around 1450. Both were forcibly removed in 1876 to the San Carlos Indian Reservation, with hundreds dying as they were marched away. About 200 Yavapai and Apache people returned in 1900 and intermingled to become the Yavapai–Apache Nation.

In modern times, spiritually open-minded migrants flock here. The primitive, healing energy of the place and the city itself, with its mix of artist communities and healers, is an irresistible pull. All have been inspired and powered by their healing, energetic surroundings.

SEDONA'S VORTEXES

In the 1960s, word began to spread among spiritual seekers to visit Sedona's "high-energy meditation sites". This was ramped up in 1982 when Page Bryant, a local psychic, said she had channelled information from the etheric realms that Sedona was the "heart chakra" of earth. She

was the first to pinpoint "vortexes": locations where earth energy is most powerful. These four vortexes – Cathedral Rock, Bell Rock, Boynton Canyon and Airport Mesa, which are all rock formations – are believed to be conducive to healing and meditation. Spiritual pilgrims come to the vortexes to be recharged and uplifted by performing yoga, meditation or rituals.

Opposite: The magical landscape of Sedona, a setting for spiritual adventures.

KNOW A THING OR TWO ABOUT: SMUDGING

This Native American tradition involves lighting the tip of a bunch of sage and letting it smoulder. The sage can be also be mixed with lavender, cedar or sweet grass. It is an act of blessing, cleansing and purification – of people and their surroundings. Some also believe it eliminates stagnant or negative energy. Sedona has numerous Native American practitioners who conduct authentic smudging ceremonies.

CRATER LAKE, KLAMATH COUNTY

OREGON, UNITED STATES

THE WONDER OF IT

Intensely blue, fathomlessly deep and profoundly still, Crater Lake has been an important sacred place for the Klamath tribes. Cloaked in myth, the lake was seen as a portal to the underworld – somewhere to be treated with respect and awe.

"There's nowhere else in the world like Crater Lake. It was one of our most sacred places. It still is."
Klamath elder

Opposite: Wizard Island, Crater Lake, considered a portal to the underworld by indigenous people.

A PORTAL BETWEEN TWO WORLDS

Crater Lake was so revered by the native Klamath people that for a long time it was only visited by shamans and chiefs: those who were physically and mentally prepared for such a mighty place. Thought to be a portal between the world of humans and the world of the spirits, it was too powerful a place for ordinary people to visit. Called Tum-sum-ne ("Mountain with the Top Cut Off"), it was where shamans vision-quested (see box, right) and undertook physical challenges to prove their spiritual powers.

The lake was seen by white men for the first time on 5 June 1853, when three gold prospectors searching for a missing colleague came across it. "This is the bluest lake we've ever seen," they said before giving it the prosaic name Deep Blue Lake. It was renamed a few times after that, eventually becoming Crater Lake. Since 1902, Crater Lake National Park has protected the deepest lake in the United States, at 592m (1,943ft), and one of the purest anywhere on earth.

The Klamath tribes have a collective memory of how it was formed more than 7,700 years ago, when Mount Mazama spectacularly erupted. Oral traditions describe "red hot rocks as large as the hills" hurtling through the sky, fire ripping through forests and the mountain collapsing into itself. The resulting caldera filled with rainwater and snow. Dazzlingly blue, sitting in the belly of the volcano, surrounded by its steep sides and ancient forests where black bear and mountain lions roam, it is a magical and uplifting place to visit. The Klamath tribes still hold ceremonies here, and it is profoundly beautiful.

There are extensive hiking routes around the lake, or you can take the 33-mile (53-km) Rim Drive by car.

In the lake near the western shore is Wizard Island, a cinder cone formed during subsequent eruptions. In summer, boat trips take visitors out to the island, a great vantage point to experience the majesty of the lake and its surrounding crater. But be warned: some geothermal activity has been recorded on the lake's floor. Mazama may erupt again!

KNOW A THING OR TWO
ABOUT: VISION QUESTS

Although primarily associated with Native American traditions, vision quests are practised by cultures all over the world. Involving spending several days alone in nature with little food, while exposed to the elements, in search of a personal vision of the future, they take place at times of significant change in an individual's life. Originally undertaken by adolescents on the brink of adulthood, they can also be performed at any times of major change, such as after a death, a birth, marriage, divorce or a house move. The purpose is to help the individual acknowledge, release and celebrate important decisions: an experience that can often be deeply cathartic.

Although it is possible to vision-quest alone, many individuals and groups can guide you through the process, make sure you come to no harm and then listen as you share the experience afterwards.

MYTHS AND MAGIC: HOW CRATER LAKE CAME INTO BEING

Llao, Chief of the Below World and spirit of the Mountain, rose from his home in the earth's belly to stand on the summit of Mount Mazama. From his lofty position, he saw the local chief's daughter and fell in love with her. He wooed her by promising eternal life if she came to his home with him. She refused and he angrily returned underground, then surged up through the mountain, threatening to kill all her people with fire and rocks.

Skell, Chief of the Above World and spirit of the Sky, saw all of this and took pity on the people. He stood on Mount Shasta (see page 166), at the other end of the Cascade Range of mountains, and challenged Llao to a fight. They battled it out, throwing large rocks at each other, causing the earth to quake and molten lava to pour until Llao was defeated and forced back into Mazama. The next day, the mountain had gone and all that remained was the crater. Some legends say that Wizard Island is actually the head of Llao.

Crawfish, a follower of Llao, is said to still inhabit the lake, waiting to grab innocent folk from the crater rim and drag them under with its long, monstrous arms. Also lurking in the waters is the Old Man of the Lake, an entire hemlock tree that floats vertically (and has done for 100 years).

Left: Crater Lake at sunrise – still, deep and profoundly beautiful.

MOUNT SHASTA, SISKIYOU COUNTY

CALIFORNIA, UNITED STATES

THE WONDER OF IT

Many are drawn to Mount Shasta and don't know why. This mighty, ice-topped cone has long been revered by Native American people and has become a spiritual focus for others in search of the sacred.

A CONE OF SPIRITUAL POWER

It's easy to see why so many legends and mysteries are associated with Mount Shasta, and why it has become a gathering place for spiritual seekers. At 4,322m (14,179ft), and with a prominence of 2,994m (9,822ft), this ice-topped, dormant volcano towers over its surroundings. Part of the Cascade Range, it is a major landmark along the Siskiyou Trail – an ancient trade and travel route based on Native American footpaths between California and the Pacific Northwest. It rises like a cone of icy power, simultaneously drawing

people close and distancing them with its awesomeness.

The mountain has long been revered by the Native American peoples. The Klamath tribe believe that it was one of the first earthly places created by the Great Spirit Skell and was his resting place after he fought Llao and created Crater Lake (see page 165). In the past, no one but a shaman climbed above the tree line – it was considered too powerful for ordinary folk.

As well as the mountain itself, the rivers, lakes and springs that surround it are equally valued by the Native Americans. Seen as places of healing and magic, they are thought to be inhabited by spirits and spirit animals. To drink and bathe in the mountain's waters is to connect with this magical realm.

To experience a little of this magic themselves, visitors flock to Headwaters Spring in Mount Shasta City Park – the origin of the Sacramento River, which gushes out of a small grotto into a shallow pool before cascading through the valley. Paths around the mountain loop through other springs (including the much-visited but lovely Panther

THE CRYSTAL CITY OF TELOS

Some people believe that a crystal city called Telos is hidden within Mount Shasta and occupied by higher-dimensional beings called Lemurians. The Lemurians are said to be part of an ancient civilization who travel through high-speed tunnels to visit other colonies around the world. They also sometimes reveal themselves to humans. A sighting during the 1940s described seeing very tall beings dressed in long white robes and sandals; they walked through town and paid for purchases in the general store with chunks of gold. There are no longer any sightings (although local mystics offer trips to vortexes on the mountain to communicate with them). However, some believe the saucer-shaped lenticular clouds that gather on the summit are created by Lemurians to camouflage alien cargo ships delivering supplies to Telos.

Meadows), waterfalls, forests and wildflower meadows. At the wellness center in Stewart Mineral Springs, located in a forested canyon in the foothills of Mount Shasta, you can soak in a mineral-rich bath, warm through in a wood-burning sauna, then plunge into the crystal-clear waters of the river.

Needless to say, there are plenty of spiritual and healing businesses in the area, offering a range of therapies including crystal singing bowls, massage, reiki, labyrinth travelling and the like. Healing retreats, campsites and sweat lodges are also on offer: spiritual tourism is a big thing here. But maybe the most powerful way to connect with the mountain and ourselves is simply to walk in its foothills and listen to its quiet presence.

Above: Mount Shasta, a cone of icy power.

"Lonely as a god, and white as a winter moon, Mount Shasta starts up sudden and solitary from the heart of the great black forests of Northern California."

Joaquin Miller, American poet and frontiersman

DEVILS TOWER
WYOMING, UNITED STATES

THE WONDER OF IT

This strange, sawn-off rock pillar looms over the plains of northeast Wyoming, a freak mountain so fantastic that it was destined to spawn legends.

A STRANGE & LONELY PILLAR

Geologists have an explanation for this peculiar, lonely rock pillar. It was formed 50 million years ago, when molten rock surged up through the earth's sedimentary bed. As the magma gradually cooled, it hardened and contracted, and in the process cracked to form a bundled stack of columns. Millions of years passed, and the surrounding soft sedimentary rock was gradually worn away, exposing the volcanic upthrust.

The native Great Plains tribes – which include the Lakota and Kiowa peoples – have a different account. Seven girls were playing in the forest when they were approached, then chased, by a huge bear. They tried to hide in a tree, but the bear still found them. They ran to a small rock, stood on it and prayed for it to save them. The Great Spirit heard them and made the rock grow higher and higher until it carried the girls into the sky. The bear still chased but it couldn't reach them no matter how high it leaped: its claws scratched deep grooves into the rock. The tower kept growing until the girls were lifted to safety.

The Lakota people call the rock Bear Lodge and come here to perform rituals, seek visions, find direction and make offerings. It is also a popular place for rock climbers, except in June when there is a voluntary climbing ban out of respect for the native people who conduct ceremonies and rituals around its base during that month.

Right: Many legends have sprung up around lonely, peculiar Devils Tower.

WIND CAVE

SOUTH DAKOTA, UNITED STATES

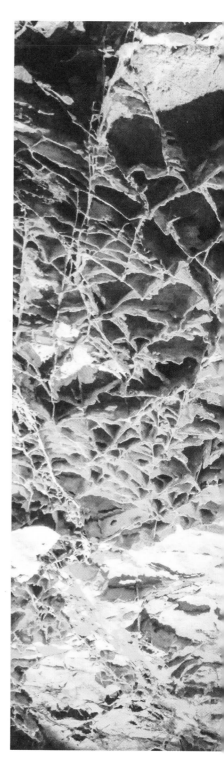

THE WONDER OF IT

Encrusted with strange calcified forms and winding its way deep into the mountains, Wind Cave has always been a place of reverence for Native American people.

A CAVE AT THE START OF THE WORLD

Above ground, buffalo still roam the prairies. Below their hooves lies a maze of passageways and caves lined with extraordinary rock formations. A place of enchantment and mystery (many of the cave's passages are yet to be explored), Wind Cave has always been a special place of reverence for Native American tribes.

To the Lakota people of the Black Hills, Wind Cave is a sacred site central to their creation story. It was where Pte Oyate (the buffalo nation) emerged from Mother Earth and became Ikce Wicasa (common people). After emergence, the Lakota saw that the Black Hills were in the shape of a buffalo, lying down, facing east. From then on, there has always

been a "sacred trust" between the Lakota and the buffalo. Buffalo appear in many Lakota stories of creation and renewal, and their spirits are called upon in ceremonies and traditions.

Wind Cave is named after atmospheric conditions that cause some passages to "breathe", as air flows from an area of low pressure to a higher one. This only adds to the magic of the place.

There is no public transport to the cave, so it's best to travel there by car (the nearest city being Rapid City) or by plane from Vancouver. Once there, take a guided tour into the throat of the cave, beneath dripping stalactites and walls encrusted with beautiful calcified rock formations that resemble honeycomb and frost, and gradually its sacred beauty is revealed.

Right: The enchanting calcite crystals in Wind Cave are known as boxwork.

HAIDA GWAII

BRITISH COLUMBIA, CANADA

THE WONDER OF IT

Far away, mystical and verdant, the islands of Haida Gwaii are the home of the Haida people, whose artistic heritage is preserved and continues to flourish to this day.

ISLANDS AT THE EDGE OF THE WORLD

It takes some determination to reach Haida Gwaii. Off the northern Pacific coast of British Columbia, across the choppy waters of Hecate Strait, this archipelago is as remote as it can get. The best way to reach these islands is by ferry from Prince Rupert.

The early people called this land Xhaaidlagha Gwaayaai or "Islands at the Boundary of the World" (later shortened to Haida Gwaii, or "land of the Haida") and, as the boat pitches and dips as you sail towards the islands, you can see why.

The isolation of Haida Gwaii, however, has been its salvation. Barely touched for centuries, it has areas of pristine temperate rainforest with some of the oldest spruce trees in the world. Nicknamed "Canada's Galapagos", it teems with wildlife, including 20 kinds of whale, dolphin and porpoise and the Haida Gwaii black bear, which exists nowhere else.

The islands are the ancestral home of the Haida people, whose oral tradition can be traced back thousands of years. Many of their early settlements have been untouched since their occupants left centuries ago – the last remains of their rich artistic heritage. Five sites can be found in the Gwaii Haanas National Park in the southernmost part of the islands, including SGang Gwaay Llnagaay (see page 174), the ancient village of Skedans on Louise Island, and the natural springs on Hotspring Island. Ancient totem poles guard where longhouses once stood, and partially carved canoes lie abandoned in the woods. The number of visitors each day is limited, ensuring that this special place is not ruined by the heavy tread of the tourist.

The number of Haida people on Haida Gwaii was devastated by a smallpox epidemic in 1862, but they still make up roughly half of the population. Haida culture thrives, especially in the towns of Old Massett and Skidegate on Graham Island, where signs are in English and Xaat Kíl, the Haida language. The Haida Heritage Centre in Kay Llnagaay near Skidegate holds dance performances in a longhouse-style theatre, and houses a collection of Haida masks, totem poles and carvings, including the Skidegate Pole by legendary Haida artist Bill Reid. Totem poles continue to be made in its Carving House. Like the natural environment that is so important to them, Haida culture and heritage look as though they are in good hands.

'When you walk this earth, you must walk carefully. Underneath your feet is the knife's edge, and you could fall off this world.'
Haida proverb

Opposite: Haida Gwaii is the remote ancestral home of the Haida people.

SGANG GWAAY LLNAGAAY

BRITISH COLUMBIA, CANADA

THE WONDER OF IT

Totem poles of the Haida people stand like sentinels, guarding an abandoned village. Left to decay naturally, they are slowly returning to the earth.

SPIRITS OF THE PAST

The Haida people occupied the village of SGang Gwaay Llnagaay on the small isle of Haida Gwaii (see page 172) for more than 8,000 years, leaving shortly after 1880, driven away by a smallpox epidemic. The village they left behind is softly returning to the earth: the timber houses and totem poles being silently reclaimed by nature. The Haida believe that the poles have a natural life like a human, so they leave them alone. They come to clean out any debris and brush away leaves, but otherwise the carved poles are left to decay naturally.

The village has the largest group of Haida totem poles in Haida Gwaii: 26 in total. These include mortuary poles where the remains of important tribe members are stored in a box at the top or at the rear. The Haida believe that when the pole finally falls back to earth, the deceased chief's spirit will be fully released.

The number of visitors to SGang Gwaay Llnagaay is capped at 12 at a time; sometimes fewer. This provides a rare and welcome opportunity to absorb the atmosphere and spirit of this sacred place. Haida watchmen take tours to the site, walking visitors through the forest, explaining the significance of the totem poles and recounting traditional stories.

It is rare to see totem poles, especially with fine carvings like these, still in their original position. Walking among them as they stand tall and wise, silvered with age, is a spiritual experience comparable to Easter Island or Stonehenge.

> SGang Gwaay Llnagaay means "red cod island". Its alternative name, Ninstints, was the name of a powerful village chief in the mid-19th century.

TOTEM POLES

These monumental carved poles (*Gyaa aang* in the Haida language) are seen across the islands of Haida Gwaii and are representations of the spirits who still guard the land. Carved from large trees like Western Red Cedar, there are six types:

1 **HOUSE FRONTAL POLE:** Located outside the house of the village leader, this is the most decorative of all poles. Its carvings tell the story of the clan which owns it.

2 **HOUSE POST:** A post that supports roof beams inside a clan house, often containing carvings that tell a story.

3 **MORTUARY POLE:** This incorporates a niche at the top to include the ashes or remains of an important individual in the community.

4 **MEMORIAL POLE:** This stands at the front of a clan house to commemorate the deceased – often a clan chief.

5 **WELCOME POLE:** This is placed at the edge of a stream or beach to welcome visitors to the community.

6 **SHAME POLE:** A shame pole is carved to ridicule individuals or groups who have transgressed.

Opposite: A mortuary pole with its hollowed-out top, SGang Gwaay Llnagaay.

BAFFIN ISLAND (QIKIQTANI)

NUNAVUT, CANADA

THE WONDER OF IT

Members of the Inuit community of Baffin Island understand how to live in the brutal but beautiful world. The rest of us can look on and marvel.

SOME INUIT BELIEFS

- Animals have the power to hear and understand human words. Inuit hunters may refer to walrus or seal as "maggots" or "lice" or call caribou "lemmings" in order to confuse them.

- There are other worlds beneath the sea, inside the earth and sky, where some *anatquqs* (shamans) can journey in trances and in dreams. They visit places ordinary mortals only experience in the afterlife.

A HARSH, BEAUTIFUL WORLD

Surrounded by a still, blue sea dotted with chunks of floating pack ice, with glaciers slowly advancing across its mountains, Baffin Island is a forlorn but beautiful place. Canada's largest island is a land where the sun never sets in summer and where the moon provides the only light in winter.

This is home to the Inuit people, who have learned to survive in its brutal conditions. Their connection to, and understanding of, the land and its creatures has meant that they have thrived where others would be defeated. This does not mean that they are oblivious to danger. They carry out rituals as precautions against unseen forces and imminent threats, often through *angakkuit* (shamans). These mediators between humans and the world of spirits have the ability to "breathe" or "blow" sickness away. An animistic belief that all things have a spirit, as well as a rich oral tradition of legends, help to make sense of the tough but magical world they inhabit.

Above: Mount Thor, Auyuittuq National Park, forlorn and beautiful.

BAFFIN ISLAND HIGHLIGHTS

INUKSUK NATIONAL HISTORIC SITE, FOXE PENINSULA: On the shore of the Northwest Passages above the high-tide line, more than 100 *inuksuit*, or stone cairns, stand on a treeless rocky hill that slopes towards the sea. Some are figures, others just one or two balanced stones. The biggest are 2m (6ft 6in) high, and some are estimated to be 2,000 years old.

AUYUITTUQ NATIONAL PARK, CUMBERLAND PENINSULA: Granite peaks, glaciers, tundra valleys and fjords, *inuksuit* – this place offers the entire Arctic experience.

KATANNILIK TERRITORIAL PARK, META INCOGNITA PENINSULA: The Soper (Kuujjuaq) Heritage River meanders more than 100km (62 miles) through the 1,262sq km (487 sq miles) of sometimes surprisingly verdant wilderness of this enormous park. Cascades tumble down the side of the valley: *Katannilik* means "waterfalls". Caribou, Arctic wolves and red foxes live here, as do lemmings and hares. Polar bears are sometimes seen on its coastal fringes.

SIRMILIK NATIONAL PARK, QIKIQTAALUK: An expansive landscape of glaciers (*Sirmilik* means "place of glaciers"), *hoodoos* (towering rocky columns) and sea cliffs, covering most of the northern tip of Baffin Island. The park is divided into three areas: the uninhabited and vast Bylot Island, the long narrow fjord, Oliver Sound, and the Borden Peninsula.

1. INUKSUK NATIONAL HISTORIC SITE, FOXE PENINSULA
2. AUYUITTUQ NATIONAL PARK, CUMBERLAND PENINSULA
3. KATANNILIK TERRITORIAL PARK, META INCOGNITA PENINSULA
4. SIRMILIK NATIONAL PARK, QIKIQTAALUK

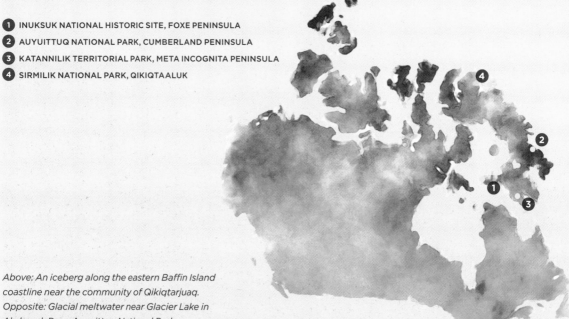

Above: An iceberg along the eastern Baffin Island coastline near the community of Qikiqtarjuaq.
Opposite: Glacial meltwater near Glacier Lake in Akshayuk Pass, Auyuittuq National Park.

MYTHS & MAGIC: INUIT LEGENDS

As westernization and global warming cause the old Inuit way of life to gradually vanish – many Inuit people have been relocated to settlements – there has been a resurgence of interest in Inuit myths and legends. The fight to keep them alive and relevant is an important part of maintaining Inuit culture. Short and dramatic, they are narratives to explain creation, natural phenomena, human behaviour, death and the afterlife, among other things. They include a cast of fabulous characters.

DEMONS

Mahaha: Tickles its victims to death with its sharp nails.

Ijiraat: Shapeshifting land-spirits that may change into Arctic animals but cannot disguise their red eyes.

Taqriaqsuit: Shadow people who are rarely seen but often heard.

Qallupilluk: Scaly marine creatures that smell of sulphur and snatch children into the sea.

GODS

Igaluk: The powerful moon god.

Malina: Igaluk's sister and the solar deity.

Nanook: The master of polar bears.

Akna: The goddess of fertility and childbirth.

Anguta: Gatherer of the dead.

THE INUKSUIT SIGNPOSTS OF THE INUIT PEOPLE

There are few landmarks on the vast Arctic landscape. Flat and featureless, its fields of tundra, snow and ice stretch endlessly ahead. Apart from, that is, mysterious stone figures that appear out of the ice-blue, breaking the horizon, creating a point of interest, showing the way ahead.

These are *inuksuit* (singular: *inuksuk*), made by the Inuit people of North America, and found in Nunavut – the most northerly territory of Canada, Greenland and Alaska. The signposts of the Arctic, they have many different meanings. Communication devices, they tell fellow travellers the route to follow, where to hunt, fish, camp, worship or store food. They can mean "you are on the right path" or "cross the river here" or "this is a food cache" or "wait here for the musk ox" or "stand here to feel the power".

Some *inuksuit* are single monolithic stones left by a solitary hunter; some are crosses or towers. Others are grander affairs, often constructed by groups of people, which resemble huge figures standing alone in the wilderness. The word *inuksuk* derives from *inuk* (person) and *suk* (substitute) and means "in the likeness of a human".

How *inuksuit* are built and how the stones are arranged reflects the unity and spirit of the Inuit people. They are constructed from the stones at hand, with each one chosen carefully to fit with the others and to support those above and below. The whole edifice is secured by balance: removal of one will destroy the lot.

Destruction of *inuksuit* is forbidden. Some have stood marking the way for centuries. These ancient inuksuit are called *tuniqtaqaliqtillugu* and are said to have been "built by those who prepared the land for our ancestors". They are timeless markers; silent messengers from the past often venerated as symbols of the ancestors.

Inuksuit continue to be built and to mark the way. They also serve as an Inuit cultural symbol: the flag of Nunavut has a red one at its centre, accompanied by a blue star representing Niqirtsuituq, the North Star.

Right, above: The official flag of Nunavut features a red inuksuk and a blue star which represents the Niqirtsuituq (the North Star).
Right: An inuksuk, *a traditional Inuit land marker.*

LE GRAND RASSEMBLEMENT

SAINTE FLAVIE, QUEBEC, CANADA

THE WONDER OF IT

Vanishing then reappearing with the tides, the lonesome figures of this art project in Quebec provoke thoughts of mortality and the human condition.

WHERE ALL SOULS WILL COLLIDE

Filing out into the Saint-Lawrence River near the village of Sainte Flavie in Quebec, 100 or so cement and wooden figures stand together but are essentially alone. This art project, Le Grand Rassemblement ("The Great Gathering"), is the work of local Canadian artist Marcel Gagnon, who runs a guesthouse and gallery nearby. The life-size figures stare ahead without expression, zombie-like. Their faces are crudely carved, and their bodies are without limbs, like individual fingers stuck into the sand. Of varying sizes, some bend slightly towards each other, but most are bolt upright, alert.

Gagnon began his creation in 1986 when he made the first 80 figures. Inspired by the movement of the tides in the river, he positioned them at various depths along the shore. At high tide, the figures are engulfed by the water, some vanishing altogether, as though they are walking towards their end. At low tide, they emerge on to solid ground. The effect is haunting, eerie and thought-provoking.

In 1992, Gagnon added a series of wooden rafts, tethered to the shore, carrying clothed wooden figures and a single sail. When the tide comes in, the rafts rise but do not float away. At low tide, they sit motionless on the sand, waiting for the tide to return.

Above: The haunting statues process out into the waters of the Saint Laurence River.

MAUNA KEA, BIG ISLAND

HAWAII, UNITED STATES

THE WONDER OF IT

This mighty volcano is so awesome, so high and so revered that it has been a no-go zone for Hawaiian native people for centuries. It still has the power to inspire deep veneration.

> Mauna Kea means "white mountain" because its slopes are covered with snow in winter.

VOLCANO OF THE GODS

These days the summit of the Mauna Kea volcano is cluttered with the white orbs of observatories trained to look at the stars. For native Hawaiians, however, it is a sacred place where you only venture with good reason.

Best admired from afar, all five volcanoes of Hawaii are revered, but Mauna Kea, the highest, is the most sacred. Measuring 10,000m (32,808ft) from its base on the sea floor to the top, and with an elevation of 4,207m (13,803ft) above sea level, it reaches up towards the celestial realm, connecting heaven and earth. The highest point of the Hawaiian Islands, it dominates all around it – it is always in view. Its barren, cinder-strewn upper slopes are considered to be Wao Akua ("the place where the gods and spirits live") – anyone from Na Kauaka ("the place of the people") has to think very carefully before going there. In the past, a *kapu* (ancient Hawaiian law) restricted visitors to high-ranking *ali'i* (rulers), although this has broadened in modern times.

Mauna Kea is also central to Hawaii's creation story. According to some oral accounts, when the Sky Father, Wākea, and the Earth Mother, Papahānaumoku, married, their union gave rise to the Hawaiian Islands and mountains. Their first-born (*hiapo*) was Big Island, and Mauna Kea was that child's *piko* (navel). To native Hawaiians, then, Mauna Kea is not just a volcano – it's the centre of existence, an umbilical cord that connects the land to the gods.

Four female deities are said to live on Mauna Kea: Poli'ahu, the snow goddess; Lilinoe, who controls the mist; Waiau, the angel of underground water; and Kane, who looks after the springs. The mountain's slopes and its *wahi pana* ("sacred places") are their terrain. Kane is associated with Lake Waiau, a small lake at an elevation of 3,968m (13,020ft), the water of which is used by native healers in ceremonies. Temples and altars are dotted about, as are burial sites: Hawaiians have been interred here for centuries.

> *"Mauna Kea was always kupuna [ancestor] to us… And there was no wanting to go to the top…It was a hallowed place…you don't need to go there. You don't need to bother it. It was the foundation of our island."*
> Kumu Pono Associates' oral history study, 1999

Opposite: Mauna Kea is revered by native Hawaiians. A white-domed observatory is just visible in the distance.

CENTRAL & SOUTH AMERICA

The countries of Central and South America have some of the most awe-inspiring sacred sites in the world. From Machu Picchu, the preserved city of the Incas cradled in the Sacred Valley of the Andes, to the Floating Islands of Lake Titicaca and the natural beauty of Costa Rica, they all have the power to transcend and uplift.

SAN JUAN TEOTIHUACÁN

VALLEY OF MEXICO, MEXICO

THE WONDER OF IT

In this ancient ruined city of great sophistication and scale, men were sacrificed and gods created the world.

WHERE MEN BECAME GODS

Even in ruins, the scale of the city of Teotihuacán is staggering. Located about 50 km (30 miles) from Mexico City, visitors walking around slack-jawed are dwarfed by the scale of the monuments that surround them. The massive stepped Pyramid of the Sun sits on a high plateau laid out in a grid of plazas, palaces and temples covering 18sq km (7 sq miles). The smaller Pyramid of the Moon, to its right, is placed at the end of the 4-km (2½-mile) Avenue of the Dead, the city's main thoroughfare, which is also lined with temples and palaces. At the other end, is the Ciudadela (Citadel), a plaza surrounded by more temples and containing the great Temple of the Feathered Serpent: Quetzalcóatl.

At its peak (around 450 CE), Teotihuacán had a population of over 125,000 people, many of whom were housed in multi-family compounds on the site. Much of the infrastructure that existed then – waterways, houses, markets – has vanished, but even so it is a spectacular example of ancient town planning. This was a busy metropolis full of the hustle and bustle of daily life, but there was a difference between it and today's modern cities: it was also a city of the gods.

Once thought to be the work of the Aztecs, Teotihuacán was actually built much earlier by a mysterious pre-Columbian people. Little is known about these original inhabitants, apart from their being fierce warriors. Prisoners captured in battle were sacrificed in their thousands as offerings to the gods so that the city would prosper. The bodies of many of these were incorporated into the structure of the temples. Animals that were considered sacred – cougars, wolves, eagles, owls – were buried alive or imprisoned in cages. Offerings of jade and obsidian have also been found.

The placement of the Pyramid of the Sun was not random: it was built over a cave shaped like a four-leaf clover. This cave was an important sacred site – it is thought to have been the place where the gods gathered to create the sun and moon after the last great catastrophe destroyed the world. In fact, nothing is random at Teotihuacán: the Avenue of the Dead runs on a north–south axis and points at the Pleiades star cluster, and all major structures are either aligned astronomically or tie in with a sacred solar calendar.

The pre-Columbian Teotihuacán flourished from about 100 BCE to 750 CE, when its buildings were sacked and burned. Who was responsible and why is a mystery, but the city was abandoned until the Aztecs arrived around 1320 CE. They immediately recognized its importance – it would have been hard not to – and made it their religious centre. They, too, saw it as the place where the gods had created the world, and gave it its name Teotihuacán, the city "where men become gods".

Opposite: All major buildings in Teotihuacán are aligned astronomically or tie in with the lunar calendar.

CUSCO, MACHU PICCHU & THE SACRED VALLEY

PERU

THE WONDER OF IT

The remains of the Inca Empire lie scattered along the Sacred Valley. Abandoned temples and cities, once lost to the jungle, are now revealed – sophisticated, secret and sacred.

CUSCO: THE NAVEL OF THE WORLD

These days, the city of Cusco, high in the Andes, is a busy, cosmopolitan city seen by visitors as a stopping-off place before they head to the Sacred Valley and Machu Picchu. For the Incan people, however, it was their capital and an important religious centre. It was also the navel of the world.

The Inca Empire was divided into four quarters (called *suyus*) and Cusco was at its centre. A series of 42 ritual pathways (*ceques*) radiated from Cusco to the rest of the empire. Along the paths were *huacas* – places of ceremonial or ritual significance, such

as springs, boulders, hidden caves or buildings.

The quarters converged in Cusco at Qorikancha, the Temple of the Sun and the most sacred Incan place. Aligned to the midwinter solstice, it was where the emperor sat on 21 June in a gem-encrusted, gold-plated recess (the entire temple was plated with gold) waiting for the sunrise. The sun shone into the recess, creating a blaze of enveloping golden light, which confirmed him as the Son of the Sun.

Qorikancha was looted and its treasures melted down within months of the Spanish conquistadors arriving in Cusco, and only a fragment of the (very fine) stonework now remains. Forming the base of a colonial church, it is worth visiting, however, to get a sense of what it was like and to stand at the navel of the Inca Empire.

Opposite: El Valle Sagradao (the Sacred Valley), the start of the Inca Trail leading to Machu Picchu.

THE SACRED VALLEY: A PEACEFUL & FERTILE PLACE WHERE INCA EMPERORS LIVED

About 15km (9 miles) north of Cusco, the valley of the Río Urubamba, a tributary of the Amazon, is a peaceful place that has been cultivated and inhabited by various civilizations since around 800 BCE. The Incan Empire took over the region in 1420 and ruled here until the arrival of the Spanish in the middle of the 16th century. It was known as a *willkamayu* (sacred river) in Quechua, the language of the Incan Empire, and thousands of *huacas* (see page 188) were scattered along its hills, rocks and streams.

This fertile valley was also where the Incan rulers lived and built temples, including Ollantaytambo, the estate of Emperor Pachacuti. Among the best-preserved Inca ruins, it was one of the few places where the Spanish conquistadors were defeated: the leader of the Inca resistance, Manco Inca, drove them back with water propelled through channels from its steep terraces. (Manco later withdrew to live in the Inca stronghold, Vilcabamba, deep in the forest.) It also marks the start of the four-day, three-night hike known as the Inca Trail, which leads to Machu Picchu.

MACHU PICCHU: THE LOST CITY OF THE INCA

One of the most spectacular, and best-known, sites in the world, this fortress city sits high in the Andes, enclosed on three sides by a steep gorge. Below it, the Río Urubamba boils and surges. On the fourth side is a mountainous ridge. As settings go, this mountaintop citadel can't be beaten. Once thought to be Vilcabamba, the last stronghold of the Inca, it is more likely to have been a royal retreat built by the first Incan emperor, Pachacuti. The number of features that align with celestial formations suggest it was also an important religious centre. Its well-preserved ruins and sacred sites offer a glimpse into the cultural and religious life of the Inca.

The city lay buried in the jungle until 1911 when an American academic and explorer, Hiram Bingham, searching for Vilcabamba, was led to it by a local man. As the undergrowth was cleared, granite walls, dizzyingly high agricultural terraces, stairways and water channels carved into the rock were revealed. There was a central plaza, a royal palace and a Temple of the Sun, a Temple of Three Windows, and a ceremonial sun dial, the Intihuatana, and all were built with astonishingly precise stonework.

Machu Picchu was abandoned shortly before the Spaniards arrived. Why everyone left is unknown: there is no evidence of violence or destruction. The conquistadors knew nothing about it and never made the journey up the mountain.

Opposite: A ceremony to honour Pachamama, revered by the indigenous people of South America.

PACHAMAMA

HER DIVINE FAMILY

In Incan mythology, Pachamama is the daughter of Viracocha, the supreme god, and the mother of Inti, the sun god, and Mama Quilla, the moon goddess.

A GODDESS FOR TODAY

The spirit of Pachamama is still very much alive today. In Peru and Ecuador, to thank and honour her, offerings and toasts (*challa*) are regularly given. In March during Martes de Challa, a small amount of chicha (a drink made from maize) is spilled on the floor as an offering to the goddess and other nature spirits (*apus*), in gratitude for the harvest, before the rest is drunk.

Although *challas* are offered to Pachamama all year, an important festival, the Challa or Pogo, takes place during the first week of August. During this, the coldest month, it is important to keep on good terms with Pachamama so she will protect livestock and crops in the year ahead. All work halts and families gather to cook a special dish (the *tijtincha*) which is then buried in a hole in the ground so Pachamama can eat it. Festivities continue all week with eating, fireworks and general celebrations, ending with a parade, where the oldest woman is elected as Pachamama Queen of the Year. This relatively recent tradition (it started in 1949) honours senior indigenous women as living symbols of wisdom, life, fertility and reproduction.

THE WONDER OF IT

Pachamama is a fertility goddess revered by the indigenous people of the Andes in Bolivia, Ecuador, Chile, Peru and northern Argentina. In the Quechuan language, Pachamama literally means "World (or Earth) Mother": she takes care of planting and harvesting, and embodies the spirit and essence of nature. She is often depicted rising from a mountain with arms full of potatoes, vegetables and fruit.

Pachamama is not entirely benevolent, however: she has the power to both sustain and destroy life on Earth. If she feels that the natural world is being abused, she will respond with a shudder that causes earthquakes.

HANAL PIXÁN, MEXICO

To the Mayan people of the Yucatán Peninsula, the human soul (*pixán*) is a gift given by the gods. After death, *pixáns* travel along pathways to the gods guided by a hairless and barkless Xoloitzcuintli, a sacred dog. At the gods' discretion, the *pixáns* then travel back along these pathways to enter a pregnant woman's womb and are reborn. The souls of the dead also make another, annual appearance: they return to visit their families during the three-day festival of Hanal Pixán.

Like the Day of the Dead (Día de Muertos) traditions in other parts of Mexico, Hanal Pixán honours and celebrates deceased family members and friends. The difference is that for Mayans, food is at the heart of the festivities: Hanal Pixán means "food for the souls".

The day before the return of the souls (31 October), families go to cemeteries to prepare their way by cleaning the graves, decorating them with yellow or purple flowers and lighting candles. Back home, altars are set up. Each is covered with an embroidered tablecloth, a green cross (representing the yaxche tree – see box below), pictures of the deceased, drink, candles, salt, a glass of water and other personal effects.

The souls of children return at midnight on 1 November during U Hanal Palal. Candles are lit to guide them home, and toys and sweets are left on the altar. The spirits of adults come the following night, on U Hanal Nucuch Uinicoob, and food and alcoholic drink, even cigarettes, are left for them. Animals are tied up to keep them out of the way of the *pixán*, and everyone goes to bed early. In some rural communities red or black string is placed around the wrists of the children to protect them from mischievous *pixán*.

As the dead have travelled a long way and will be hungry, an additional, special dish – *mucbil pollo* – is also prepared. Unique to the Mayan people, this is similar to a tamale – pieces of chicken (or rabbit or pork) wrapped in a corn dough, then enclosed in banana leaves. The *mucbil pollo* is cooked in an underground pit called a *pib*, although some are taken to a bakery or cooked at home in the oven. Once cooked, it is placed on the altar for the souls to eat. What is left is enjoyed later by the living. A plate of food is also put out for Lonely Souls who don't have anyone to remember them.

On the third day, U Hanal Pixanoob, a mass is said for the souls of the dead, usually in the cemetery.

Above: A Mexican death angel .
Opposite: Painted dancers with Catrina skulls for Day of the Dead at Festival de las Animas.

KNOW A THING OR TWO ABOUT: YAXCHE – THE MAYAN TREE OF LIFE

The *yaxche* ("green tree" or "first tree") is central to the Mayan creation story and culture. According to Popol Vuh, an ancient Mayan scripture, the gods planted four Ceiba trees in each corner of the world to hold up the heavens. The fifth tree was planted in the centre so its roots could reach the underworld and its branches could reach the heavens. This *yaxche*, Tree of Life, connected the three realms – the heavens, middle world and underworld – and was a channel between humans and gods. The formation of the five trees (known as a *quincunx*) is often seen in Mayan architecture and art. Its symbol – a green cross – is part of the celebrations at Hanal Pixán and displayed on altars.

The Ceiba tree flourishes in the rainforests of Mexico. It can grow up to 70m (230ft) tall and has a straight trunk, "buttressed" roots and no lower branches: they are bunched at the top in an umbrella-like canopy. A worthy tree to represent the Tree of Life.

FIVE SOUTH AMERICAN FESTIVALS

1 FEBRUARY – FESTIVAL DE LA CANDELARIA, PUNO, PERU: This fusion of Catholicism and traditional beliefs celebrates the patron saint of Puno, the Virgen de la Candelaria, with events that last several days. On 2 February at 2pm, following a mass, the statue of the Virgin is paraded through the streets. As many as 50,000 dancers in elaborate costumes fill the streets with colour and movement. Prizes are given to the best. Offerings are also made to Pachamama for a fruitful harvest. A similar festival also takes place in Copacabana, Bolivia.

2 FEBRUARY – CARNAVALE DE ORURO, BOLIVIA: Six days of celebration including the Anata Andino, a ritual giving thanks to Pachamama for a good harvest. Men, women and children embellish their traditional clothes with flowers and other produce and dance to Jallu Pacha music. The city is also decorated with flowers. In the evening the *challas*, a ritual of thanks to Pachamama, takes place: the earth is sprinkled with wine, and fireworks announce that the *wajt'a* (an offering) will be burnt to honour her. On the day of the main procession, more than 50,000 dancers take to the streets all day, some dressed as devils to perform the Diablada (the dance between good and evil).

3 EASTER WEEK – SEMANA SANTA, ANTIGUA, GUATEMALA: During Easter week, the streets of Antigua are transformed as the people create *alfombras* – carpets of sand, sawdust and flowers – along the Good Friday processional route. These intricate, ephemeral designs are the products of months of planning for the Catholic festival. Floats which re-enact the last days of Christ are carried by *cucuruchos* (float-bearers) wearing purple, as clouds of incense billow around them. The *cucuruchos* are the only ones allowed to walk over the *alfombras*, which they do with measured footsteps as the procession makes its way on.

4 JUNE – INTI RAYMI (FESTIVAL OF THE SUN), CUSCO, PERU: Started in the early 1400s, this festival honours Inti, the sun god of the Incas, with processions, dances and rituals. Banned by the Catholic Spaniards in 1536, it was revived in 1994 when a film crew staged a reconstruction. Centred around the Inca site of Sacsayhuamán above Cusco, it is now a finely choreographed spectacle attracting many (fee-paying) tourists. An actor is chosen to portray Sapa (the emperor) who is carried on a golden chariot from Qorikancha temple to Sacsayhuamán. Rituals and the symbolic (simulated) sacrifice of two llamas call back the sun on what is the winter solstice, the shortest day of the year. The Sapa also raises a cup of *chicha* (an alcoholic drink) before pouring it as an offering to Inti.

5 OCTOBER – SEÑOR DE LOS MILAGROS (LORD OF THE MIRACLES), LIMA, PERU: One of the largest Catholic processions in Latin America originates in the 17th century, with an image of the Crucifixion painted by an Angolan slave on a wall of the Church of Las Nazarenas. Despite a violent earthquake in the 18th century which destroyed most of the city, it remained intact. Every year, thousands of Catholics walk through the streets of Lima, in what has become the main Catholic celebration in Peru and one of the largest processions in the world. Members of the Lord of the Miracles Brotherhood carry the 13-kg (28-lb) artwork through the streets, accompanied by women in purple dresses and men wearing purple ties.

Clockwise from top left: An Aymara woman dancing during festival season; Actors dressed as Inca soldiers carrying the Inca Queen at Inti Raymi; A Holy Week carpet (alfombra) *made using wooden stencils and dyed sawdust for Semana Santa; A devil dancer during carnival.*

CHICHÉN ITZÁ
& CENOTE SAGRADO

YUCATÁN PENINSULA, MEXICO

THE WONDER OF IT

Staggering in its scale, its astronomical complexity and the beauty of its carvings and murals, the city of Chichén Itzá also has a bloody, sacrificial past.

IN TUNE WITH THE COSMOS

The Mayan people were deeply religious and worshipped gods related to elements of nature such as the sun, moon, rain and corn. Much of their success with agriculture, pottery and mathematics they credited to good relationships with their deities. To honour the gods and keep in their favour, they constructed immense temples and cities where they would gather to make offerings, give thanks and pray. Nowhere is this more evident than at the great ceremonial city of Chichén Itzá, a complex of ruins on Mexico's Yucatán Peninsula.

The name means "at the mouth of the well of Itza". (*Chi* means "mouth", *chen* means "well" and *itza* refers to the tribe that settled there.) Water was central to the choice of location of the city; the limestone plain on which the city was built has no rivers, streams or ponds. The four natural sink holes (called cenotes) were the only water source. The largest of these, Cenote Sagrado (see page 198) was venerated as a sacred well, a plumb line to the underworld.

The city is dominated by the Temple of Kukulkan, also known by its Spanish name, El Castillo. The four sides of this pyramid each face in a cardinal direction. In total there are 365 steps, the number of days in the year. An hour before sunset at the two equinoxes, sunlight casts seven triangular shadows along the western balustrade of the main staircase. This creates the effect of a giant serpent's body, which joins a carved serpent's head at the bottom. Kukulkan is the feathered serpent, also known as Quetzalcoatl, a major god of the Toltec people, who introduced the cult into Mayan cities.

To the east of the Temple of Kukulkan is the Temple of the Warriors, another vast stepped pyramid surrounded by rows of columns depicting warriors, once supporting a roof. At the top of the staircase, at the entrance to a temple, is a *chac-mool*: a reclining figure (probably a fallen warrior) supporting a bowl or disc on its stomach, where sacrifices took place. It is said that priests would split open the chests of victims and offer their still-beating hearts to the gods.

Ritual and sport were combined in the fierce ball game known as *tlachtli*, played at an impressive sports pitch shaped like a capital letter I (with serifs). Players used their elbows, knees and hips to knock a solid latex ball through one of two stone rings. The ball represented the sun, and the rings stood for the sunrise and sunset of the equinoxes. Taken very seriously, the game often ended in violence, with the losing team sacrificed and decapitated.

Chichén Itzá continued to thrive as the Mayan civilization came to an end. Most Mayan stone cities had been constructed during its classic period (250–900 CE), after which much of the Mayan empire went into a mysterious decline. In the Yucatán

Peninsula, however, life went on, and at Chichén Itzá, new structures continued to be built before it was abandoned in the 1400s.

CENOTE SAGRADO (SACRED WELL)

Connected to Chichén Itzá by a 300m (984ft) *sacbe*, or raised path, this large – 60m (197ft) in diameter – and fathomless well was a place of pilgrimage for the ancient Mayan people. They came here to pay tribute to Chaac, the rain god (important for agriculture and life in general) by making offerings. Archaeological dives in recent years have uncovered thousands of objects buried in the mud at the bottom of the cenote. The more valuable the object, the greater the sacrifice and the subsequent benefits – gold, jade, pottery and textiles have been found, as well as, more ominously, a large number of human remains.

Many of the victims thrown into the cenote were boys, but there were also bones of girls, warriors and people with deformities, all killed before they were thrown in. The Mayans may have believed that the well took its victims straight to the underworld. On occasions, a particular type of algae with red seeds turns the water of the cenote the colour of blood: a morbid nod to its gruesome past. Only sacred cenotes were used this way – the other cenote at Chichén Itzá was strictly a water supply.

Previous page: Temple of Kukulkan, the four-sided pyramid in Chichén Itzá. Above: One of the stone ring 'goal' hoops on the wall of the Great Ball Court in Chichén Itzá, where the game of Pok-a-Tok was played by the Mayans. Opposite: Cenote Sagrado, with its pellucid waters and hanging roots.

LAKE TITICACA
& THE UROS
FLOATING ISLANDS

BOLIVIA / PERU

THE WONDER OF IT

It comes as no surprise that Lake Titicaca, sitting high in the Andes, vast, deep and cerulean blue, is sacred to the indigenous people who live around its shores. According to Incan mythology, this is where the god Viracocha rose to shape the world and all its inhabitants. A powerful place of creation and spirituality, it is the womb of civilization.

THE LAKE & ITS FLOATING ISLANDS

Straddling the border between Bolivia and Peru, Lake Titicaca sits on a high plateau enclosed by the dizzying, snow-topped Andes and the wild scrub of the Altiplano ("high plain"). If the thin air at this altitude – 3,812m (12,507ft) – doesn't take your breath away, the lake's vast expanse of dazzling blue water mirroring the cloudless sky will do so.

Central to Incan mythology, Lake Titicaca is where Viracocha, the Creator God, emerged to shape the world and the universe (see page 203). Traces of Inca and pre-Inca civilizations can still be found on its islands, where sacrifices and ceremonies honouring Viracocha were held in maze-like temples.

The people of Lake Titicaca have adapted to cope with the altitude and the sparse and stony terrain. Their lung capacity is a third greater here, and their heartbeat is slower. Forced to be resourceful when the Incan Empire expanded and propelled them from their land centuries ago, the Uros people found a clever way to survive: they built a floating island community from the totora reed that grew around the lake.

Totora grows here, reaching up to 6m (20ft) high, and is strong and durable enough to fashion into floating platforms, homes, boats and furniture. The Uros Islands are about 1–2m (3–6ft) thick and usually, although not always, tethered by rope or anchored by eucalyptus trunks to the bottom of the lake.

As the reeds rot and disintegrate, more reeds are added to the surface. This creates a springy but strong and buoyant surface on which to build homes. There are over 100 islands, none more than 27m (89ft) wide. The larger islands house up to 10 families, and the biggest of all has a watch tower. Some have solar panels and there is a radio station.

These days the Uros people make their living from fishing and tourism: boats leave from either side of the lake taking visitors to the larger islands, where they buy handicrafts made from – you guessed it – totora.

Opposite: The floating Uros islands on Lake Titicaca, built from the buoyant totora reeds that grow abundantly in the shallows of the lake.

ISLA DEL SOL &
ISLA DE LA LUNA
BOLIVIA / PERU

ISLA DEL SOL

The Isla del Sol, or "Island of the Sun", at the southern end of Lake Titicaca (the Bolivian part), is packed with Inca and pre-Inca (Aymaran) ruins and suffused with legend.

According to one, the Inca founder and king, Manco Cápac, and his wife, Mama Ocllo, were brought here from the depths of the lake by the sun god, Inti (son of Viracocha, see right). Another states that Viracocha emerged from a sandstone outcrop shaped like a puma at the northern tip of the island, which gave the island its original name – Titi Qala ("rock of the puma") – and the lake its current title. Human and animal sacrifices were said to have been made on the Mesa de Sacrificio, a stone slab. The Huellas del Sol, huge foot-shaped prints leading away from the village of Challapampa, are credited to Viracocha, who is said to have planted them there as he walked away to create the world.

Isla del Sol is the largest island on Lake Titicaca – it is home to several small Aymara communities – but a peaceful one. There is no traffic or Tarmac roads and it is easy to find a quiet path leading through small villages past cultivated terraces, eucalyptus trees and cacti, to the many and varied ruins. The largest of these is Chincana (meaning "a place where one gets lost"). It contains the Palacio del Inca, a labyrinthine tangle of rooms, corridors and tiny doorways which also houses a sacred well, believed to produce purifying water. Other wells are found elsewhere on the island, including the Fountain of Youth in the village of Yumani in the south. Reached by climbing 200 steep stone stairs built by the Incas, the fountain has three separate spouts, referred to as Ama Sua, Ama Kella and Ama Llulla ("Don't be lazy. Don't be a liar. Don't be a thief"), the three Inca laws.

These ancient sacred sites are still honoured by the Aymara people, who gather on the solstices to celebrate the rising sun. Ceremonies are conducted by Yatiri priests – shamans who act as intermediaries between this world and the world of the spirits. Offerings of herbs, flowers and dried llama foetus are laid out as they wait for the sun to appear. When it does, musicians play and everyone shares coca leaves and good wishes.

ISLA DE LA LUNA

According to Inca mythology, the Isla de la Luna, or "Island of the Moon", is where Viracocha commanded the moon to rise. It is considered to be the home of Mama Quilla, the moon goddess, who was Viracocha's daughter and the sister and wife of Inti (the sun god). Mama Quilla looks after women's interests, such as marriage, childbirth and menstruation. The well-preserved ruins of the Temple of the Virgins are said to be where nun-like women lived, leading a devotional life weaving garments and performing ceremonies dedicated to the sun. Small enough to walk around in a couple of hours, the island is a place of female (lunar) energy, in contrast to the Isla del Sol, which is masculine. Home to a few farming families, the Isla de la Luna is less inhabited and less touristy than the Isla del Sol.

ISLA AMANTANÍ

This circular island has two mountain peaks: Pachatata ("Father Earth") and Pachamama ("Mother Earth"), with a temple apiece honouring each. The temples are usually closed,

except on 20 January, a feast day, when local people split into two groups and visit the temple that has meaning for them. A climb to the top, past terraced fields where farmers work by hand (there are no machines on the island), will reward you with a spectacular view of Lake Titicaca, especially at sunset. Silent three-day meditation retreats are also held here around the time of the full moon.

Above: Isla del Sol on Lake Titicaca is packed with legends. Its Incan and pre-Incan ruins are still held sacred today.

MYTHS & MAGIC: VIRACOCHA

There are various legends associated with Lake Titicaca but they all centre on Viracocha, the Creator God, who ascended from its waters to bring light and shape the world.

At the start of time, when all was darkness, Viracocha rose from Lake Titicaca to bring light. From the Isla del Sol he made the sun; from the Isla de la Luna, he made the moon; and from the Isla Amantaní, he made the stars. Then, by breathing light into stones, he made a race of giants. Because there was no light, these giants stumbled around in the darkness and achieved nothing, so Viracocha sent a storm to wipe them out. The next time he used clay to form Manco Capac and Mama Ocllo (the Adam and Eve of the Andes) and gave them language, songs and clothes. He also made animals and plants. Once this was done, he dressed as a beggar and wandered the earth teaching his creations farming and other skills necessary to start civilization.

CACHOEIRA SANTUÁRIO (SANCTUARY WATERFALL)

PRESIDENTE FIGUEIREDO, BRAZIL

THE WONDER OF IT

One of many spectacular waterfalls in the Amazonian rainforest, this is a place to swim, marvel and soak up the uplifting spirit.

UPLIFTING CASCADES

To experience waterfalls in all their sublime, energizing glory, you need to switch on your senses. These waterfalls are primordial places of thunderous noise, movement and thrilling sensations that demand attention. You need to spend time beside one, walk behind its mighty cascade and swim in its pools, to soak up its life-affirming spirit.

There's no better place to seek waterfalls than inland Brazil. With its high annual rainfall, mighty rivers and dramatic changes in elevation, this is a land of tumultuous cascades, some among the largest in the world.

Cachoeira Santuário is not the most spectacular waterfall, but it is one of the loveliest. A two-hour drive from Manaus takes you to Presidente Figueiredo, which calls itself Terra de Cachoeiras ("Land of Waterfalls"). There are more than 100 waterfalls in the area, tumbling into tributaries that feed into the Rio Negro. Cachoeira Santuário, on the Urubuí River, is reached by a 15-minute walk through the jungly rainforest – a soul-soothing excursion in itself – and is part of a large ecological reserve. Surrounded by lush vegetation and mossy rocks, this is a magical place, especially in rainy season when the volume of water is high. Stand behind the waterfall and feel its power or plunge into the water for an exhilarating swim.

Opposite: the thunderous drop of water at Cachoeira da Fumacinha.

FIVE OTHER LEAST-VISITED BRAZILIAN WATERFALLS

1 **CACHOEIRA DO MACAQUINHO, CHAPADA DOS VEADEIROS:** Swim under a series of falls to reach a beautiful cave, or jump into a gin-clear pool from a 9m (30ft) ledge.

2 **CACHOEIRA DOS DRAGOES, PIERENOPOLIS:** Eight waterfalls near a Buddhist monastery are maintained by the monks, who will give tours and explain the mythology behind each.

3 **CACHOEIRA DO TORORÓ, BRASILIA:** A secluded waterfall in a small clearing close to the city centre.

4 **POÇO DA USINA, PARATY:** A small and lovely waterfall tumbles into a still pool, making this a perfect place to swim.

5 **CACHOEIRA DA FUMACINHA, CHAPADA DIAMANTINA, IBICOARA:** a 10-km (6-mile) hike takes you to a massive canyon into which water falls from a height of 250m (820ft).

LA ARAUCANÍA REGION

CHILE

THE WONDER OF IT

This land of volcanoes, hot springs, lakes and virgin forests is valued by the indigenous Mapuche people, who maintain a deep connection with the earth.

A VOLATILE & MYTHIC LAND

The indigenous Mapuche people of Araucanía in Chile believe that a harmonious relationship between people, animals and Mother Earth (Nuke Mapu) is the basis of life. The word Mapuche means people (*che*) of the land (*mapu*), and respect for their natural surroundings is central to their beliefs.

The land they care for and value is verdant, beautiful and volatile. It has six active volcanoes, including Volcán Villarrica, the highest, and one of Chile's most active. In the Mapuche language, Mapudungun, it is called Rucapillán – "devil's house". Tourists climb its steep, snow-covered sides to the crater and dodge bubbling pits of molten rock before noxious fumes send them back down again.

In Mapuche creation mythology, the bad-tempered serpent Kai Kai created the volcanoes and the lakes that surround them with an angry swipe of his hefty tail. His kindly counterpart, the serpent Tren Tren, meanwhile kept the people safe on a nearby mountain.

These days most of Araucanía's natural attractions are kept safe in national parks. The Villarrica-Hualalafquén National Reserve, site of Volcán Villarrica, also has settlements of Mapuche communities, who live among its lagoons and snow-covered mountains. Another active volcano, Volcán Llaima, is in Conguillío National Park, as well as many lakes, deep canyons and native trees often draped in lime-green moss. In Huerquehue National Park, ancient and spindly Araucaria (monkey puzzle trees) tower above deep emerald lagoons, rivers and hot springs.

More hot springs are found in Puyehue National Park, where a hot outdoor and very hot indoor pool are filled with natural healing waters.

There are more than 120 Mapuche communities, many of whom live in indigenous *reducciones* (reservations). They continue to maintain and promote Mapuche traditions, culture and language. *Machi* (shamans), often women, perform ceremonies to cure sickness and encourage a good harvest or decent weather, using their knowledge of herbal remedies, sacred stones and sacred animals, to ease both body and *lawen* (soul). At the We Tripantu festival at the June winter solstice, the return of the sun is celebrated as Nuke Mapu is fertilized by Antu, the sun god. People gather to eat, drink and tell stories until dawn, when they head down to the streams and rivers to wash away any bad things that have happened or may occur in the future.

To get a taste of Mapuche life, visitors can stay in the village of Llaguepulli, an ethnic tourist site that offers accommodation in a *ruka* (Mapuche traditional house), food and artistic and cultural activities.

Opposite above: Volcán Villarrica, known as Rucapillan, "devil's house", in the Mapuche language.
Opposite below: A machi *(shaman) playing a cultrun (ceremonial drum).*

CAVE OF THE CRYSTAL SEPULCHRE (ACTUN TUNICHIL MUKNAL CAVE)

BELIZE

THE WONDER OF IT

Inside a difficult-to-reach labyrinthine cave system lie the skeletons of 14 children and adults, all of whom reached a violent end, though their calcified remains still sparkle.

A PORTAL TO THE UNDERWORLD

You have to be prepared for quite a journey to reach this mysterious cave in the Tapir Mountain Nature Reserve in Belize. An hour's drive from San Ignacio, followed by another hour's walk through the jungle, takes you to its entrance. The only way to gain access is to swim in. Once inside, a world of huge boulders and cavernous rooms opens up. A further walk of around 1km (⅔ mile) along a river passage takes you to the final destination: a cave filled with the calcified skeletons of 14 sacrificed children and adults.

The inaccessibility of the cave and the calcification of the skeletons has meant they have remained untouched since they were deposited at this, their final resting place more than 1,000 years ago. The victims, who were Mayans aged between one year and 45 years, are scattered about in a higgledy-piggledy fashion, tossed into smaller caves or thrown on the ground without ceremony. Some of the skulls of the younger ones are deformed, as though they have been deliberately shaped. Almost all were killed by a severe blow to the head with a blunt instrument.

The most arresting, and affecting, skeleton of all is found a little farther in. The remains of an 18-year-old girl lie on the ground, her arms and legs thrown wide apart, her body twisted, her mouth agape. Two of her vertebrae have been crushed. There is little doubt that she died a violent death. Her bones have lain here for around 1,100 years, during which time they have become completely calcified. As a result, she sparkles in the light, a quality that has earned her the nickname The Crystal Maiden.

Ceramic pots used for ceremonial purposes also lie calcified on the floor, and altars have been created in the walls of the cave. Some formations have been carved to resemble faces and animals. This was obviously a place of religious significance to the Mayan people, but why it was a repository for sacrificial victims is open to speculation. The most common theory is that they were killed to appease Chac, the rain god, perhaps during a period of drought. Local people are still wary of this place, referring to it as Xibalba, "the place of fear", the underworld, ruled by Mayan death gods.

For those brave enough to enter this portal to hell, authorized guides lead tours. To avoid large groups, hire a private guide and get there early in the morning to really experience its power and to ponder its brutal past.

Opposite: The entrance to the Actun Tunichil Muknal cave which contains Mayan artefacts including a glittering skeleton of a girl.

COSTA RICA

AN ABUNDANT & MAGICAL LAND

Wild and alive, Costa Rica is a land of natural wonderment. A mystical place of impenetrable jungle, cloud forests, active volcanoes, white, black and pink beaches and mineral hot springs, it's home to the jaguar, iguana, three-toed sloth, alligator and quetzal bird. Its lush and abundant plant life includes 900 species of flowering plants.

Protecting all of this beauty is not just beneficial to the environment and its people, it is also vital to tourism. The country's government, recognizing the value of its natural assets, works hard to look after them: more than one quarter of the country is part of a protected national park. As a result, Costa Rica is the place to go to slip into the rhythm and flow of the natural world. It is easy to be transformed here: simply leave the resorts behind and walk into its abundant and magical heart.

Costa Rica's indigenous people have always had a profound appreciation of their land. Before the Spanish Conquest, there were as many as 25 different tribes, and many still remain. The Chorotegas are the largest and are known for their agricultural prowess and ceramic skills. Every year, the Boruca (Brunka) tribe still celebrates the Fiesta de los Diablitos, a three-day festival marking their resistance and cultural survival against the Spanish Conquistadors. Masked *diablitos* (ancestral spirits) take on a bull (symbolizing the Spanish) in a fight to the finish. Landmarks still carry native names. The Poás Volcano is known by indigenous people as Sibú Mountain – "Creator of Life and Wisdom"; Irazú Volcano gets its name from the indigenous word meaning "thunder and earthquake mountain". Native traditions and myths are never far away.

Unsurprisingly, eco communities and healing and wellness centres are plentiful. The country, with its slogan Pura Vida ("the pure life"), is the place to head for yoga, meditation, healing and spirituality-focused retreats. The town of Nosara and the Nicoya Peninsula are in a "blue zone" (where people live longer than anywhere else on the planet); this is where to find many of these retreats. And every February, the Envision Festival, held in the jungles of the southern Osa Peninsula, is a transformational celebration of music, dance, yoga and healthy living.

THE STONE SPHERES (LAS BOLLAS) OF DIQUÍ

Over 300 petrospheres – ancient, perfectly shaped limestone spheres – are scattered throughout Costa Rica, but especially in the south on the Delta del Diquís, Osa Peninsula and Isla del Caño. Hefty – they weigh up to 15 metric tonnes (16 Imperial tons) – their sizes vary from 10cm (4in) to 2.6m (8½ft) in diameter. Dating from around 600 CE, they are thought to be the work of a pre-Columbian people, who created them by hammering at the stone with rocks. Their significance is uncertain, but they could have been markers along a path – to a house of a chief, perhaps. They don't give much away, so they will remain a mysterious relic of Costa Rica's ancient history.

"We need the tonic of wildness."
Henry David Thoreau

THE WONDER OF IT

In this untamed and unspoilt country, the traditions of the native people are never far away, and living a simple and happy life is within everyone's grasp.

Opposite: Venture into Costa Rica's abundant and magical heart and slip into the rhythm of the natural world.

Opposite: Arenal Volcano, one of Costa Rica's active volcanoes.
Above top: The San Luis Waterfall in Monteverde, surrounded by rainforest.
Above: The Rualdo, also known as the golden-browed chlorophonia.

MYTHS AND MAGIC: THE LEGEND OF THE RUALDO BIRD

A young girl who lived near the Poás Volcano was out exploring when she was befriended by a Rualdo bird, who followed her everywhere. The little bird was a rather drab specimen with plain plumage, but it had an exquisite song. The girl's father, the village shaman, was worried the volcano was about to erupt and destroy the village, so he walked to its crater to ask how he could appease it. The spirit of the volcano said he would have to sacrifice his daughter. Although this filled him with dismay, he realized it was the only way to save his people, so he agreed. When he told his daughter she protested and had to be dragged to the volcano kicking and screaming. As she perched on the volcano's rim, the Rualdo bird appeared, flew into the crater and sang with all its might. Then it pleaded with the spirit of the volcano to exchange his song for the girl's life. Its song was so beautiful that the volcano cried – its tears filled the crater (known today as the Botos Lagoon) – and the little girl was spared. True to its pact, the bird lost its song but gained beautiful plumage of blue green and gold instead.

SAUT-D'EAU

MIREBALAIS, HAITI

THE WONDER OF IT

This waterfall in the Haitian jungle is where the sick and needy come to ask the Virgin Mary and Vodou spirits for help, and to be purified in its crashing waters.

THE SPIRITS OF THE WATERFALL

Every July, pilgrims travel to a waterfall in the jungle of Haiti to be purified and to seek blessings from the Virgin Mary and from Vodou spirits (see right). On arrival, they expose themselves to the thunderous healing water. Some wash themselves with leaves, others fall into the water, staggering, trembling and shaking. Candles are carried, drums are struck, songs are sung in Creole, and rum is drunk. It is an intoxicating scene of spiritual abandonment.

Saut-d'Eau has been considered a place of pilgrimage since 1849, when a female spirit appeared on a leaf of a palm tree near the waterfall. As the tree dropped the leaf, the image of

the spirit appeared on another. This phenomenon soon attracted people who left offerings and prayers. A Catholic priest, disapproving of this superstitious behaviour, cut the tree down. (It was rumoured that he died mysteriously later that day.) The spirit reappeared on a second tree, and the pilgrims kept coming. Eventually, a church was built nearby, and the Catholic Church declared that the vision on the leaf was that of the Virgin Mary of Mount Carmel.

This fusion of beliefs is common in Haiti. Slaves shipped here from West Africa were forced to convert to Catholicism and to abandon their own belief system of ancestor spirits. The spirits didn't go away, however – they continued to be worshipped underground in Vodou ceremonies, or became merged with Christian saints.

At Saut-d'Eau, the Virgin is honoured alongside the Vodou *loa* (spirit) Èrzulie Dantòr. Èrzulie is the spirit of motherhood and goddess of rivers, lakes and waterfalls. Prayers are made to her to cure infertility. The sick and needy let the waters fall over them and perform various rituals, hoping that she will hear them and help.

KNOW A THING OR TWO ABOUT: VODOU

Vodou is a blend of beliefs derived from the tribal cults of West Africa, brought to Haiti by slaves. Along the way it soaked up many elements of Catholicism and bits of ceremonial from textbooks of the ritual magic of 18th-century France. Although Vodouists believe in one god, Bondye, he is distant and unreachable, and communication is through spirits called *loa*. These include Baron Samedi, Lord of the underworld, who watches over cemeteries; Papa Legba who is an intermediary between the *loa* and humanity and is associated with dogs; and Èrzulie Dantòr, a female spirit who protects children and is the goddess of rivers, lakes and waterfalls. During rituals, *loa* are invited to possess individuals, while animal sacrifices are made to appease the spirits.

Opposite above: A Haitian boy performs the purification ritual at Saut-D'Eau.
Opposite below: Pilgrims at the waterfall – a scene of spiritual abandonment.

INDEX

PICTURE CREDITS

Page 14–15: Ad Deir Monastery, in the rock city of Petra, Jordan.
Pages 40–1: A stone dragon guards Wat Pra That Lampang Luang, Thailand.
Pages 84–5: Mitre Peak, New Zealand, an important site for the Ngai Tahu people.
Pages 108–9: The dramatic Reynisfjara black sand beach, Iceland.
Pages 152–3: Could Cathedral Rock in Sedona, Arizona, be an energy vortex?
Pages 184–5: The Uros islands, made from totora reeds, Peru.
Page 224: The path to Aoraki, New Zealand.

An Hachette UK Company
www.hachette.co.uk

First published in Great Britain in 2020 by Aster,
an imprint of Octopus Publishing Group Ltd
Carmelite House
50 Victoria Embankment
London EC4Y 0DZ
www.octopusbooks.co.uk

Text copyright © Clare Gogerty 2020

Distributed in the US by Hachette Book Group,
1290 Avenue of the Americas, 4th and 5th Floors,
New York, NY 10104

Distributed in Canada by Canadian Manda Group,
664 Annette St., Toronto, Ontario, Canada M6S 2C8

ISBN 978 1 78325 335 7

A CIP catalogue record for this book
is available from the British Library.

Printed and bound in Malaysia

10 9 8 7 6 5 4 3 2 1

Consultant Publisher: Kate Adams
Senior Managing Editor: Sybella Stephens
Copy Editor: Alison Wormleighton
Senior Designer Jaz Bahra
Designer: Megan van Staden
Picture Research Manager: Jennifer Veall
Assistant Production Manager: Lucy Carter

The information contained in this book is for general
information purposes only. While the information was
correct at the time of going to print, we make no
representations or warranties of any kind about the
completeness, accuracy, reliability, suitability or availability
with respect to the locations or related maps for any purpose.